Let's Not Call It Meditation:

Practical guidance for people who think they can't sit still

and

quiet the mind

Let's Not Call It Meditation

Practical guidance
for people
who think
they can't sit still
and
quiet the mind

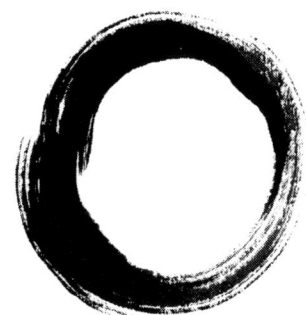

by Padme Nina Livingstone

© 2006 by Padme Nina Livingstone

All rights reserved. This book, or parts thereof, may not be reproduced in any form without permission except for brief quotations embodied in critical articles and reviews.

Printed in the United Sates of America.

ISBN 0-9788351-0-7

This work goes out

with the prayer

that

this writing be useful,

in some way,

to all readers.

An Invitation

The vision.

Imagine an open-ended body of water, stretching out from land. Several people stand along the shore. They are barefoot, with their toes facing the water. Some have taken a few steps in and gotten their feet wet. Most are standing along the edge where the quiet water meets the beach.

All eyes are on a smiling woman standing in the water ahead of them. I am the woman. I am speaking about how awareness helps us deepen our life experience so that we can be awake and present to all life brings our way. Everyone listening is invited to find out how meditation develops more awareness. The water in the vision represents awareness deepened by a meditation practice.

Feeling joyful and clear, I call to the people on shore, inviting them to join me. "Come on in. The water's fine!"

I later understood that the people on shore represent readers of this book. Some have already stepped into the water, but are not sure they want to keep going. They are drawn to going deeper, but are cautious, yet interested enough to not walk away.

Others have heard about this place but have never visited here before. They are curious about the possibility of change that lies before them. In the vision these people feel unsure. They put a toe in the water. Then take it out. Then try again.

In addition, the people who have stepped into the water are deciding how deep they want to go. They are wondering to themselves, "Am I deep enough? Should I keep going?"

The purpose of this book is to help people connect with their longing for an awake, joyful life, by passing on what one person has learned from direct experience about awareness and meditation. The title suggests that dropping the word "meditation" is an opportunity to bypass any misconceptions, fears, or reservations about meditation. This whole book is an invitation to think of meditation as a practice we can do to help us find the happiness we want, a practice that gives us the real possibility of having a healthy, balanced, compassionate, and joyful life.

"Come on in. The water's fine."

An Invitation...ix

Contents

Preface...page 17
What do we really want?...Seeking happiness, avoiding pain...
Wanting it to be easy...Patti's Story...What's in a word...You are invited

Part I: Remembering Who We Long To Be

Illustration: The Flowering of Inner Growth

Chapter One: Seven Key Elements for Growth ...page 29

1. Intention: A love triangle... Good Intentions help develop discretion... Learning the hard way...Wanting nothing...Feeling open to everything

2. Longing: A personal story...Jackie's story

3. Energy: Shifting attitude, shifting Energy...Finding the Balance... Active Curiosity... When pain is *all that is*

4. Roots of Confusion: Untangling confusion

5. Light of Awareness: Being with *what is*... Autobiography in Five Short Chapters...A family mess

6. Desire for Change: Inevitability of change...Opening to change... Naming Practice...Personal check-in

7. Balance: The working world...Balance and Chaos... Questions to ponder

Chapter Two: The Flower's Six Petals...page 81

Blossoming into our wholeness

1. Curiosity: Three and a half hours late

2. Humor: Who's hearing now...Shopping spree...
From Harper's Index...The drive for success...Four moms...Zen hot dog

3. Gratitude: Painful stuff...Turning the compost

4. Compassion: Opening the way...Our stories...
Ray Charles...Expanding our view

5. 100% Responsibility: Forgiving the boss

6. Creativity: Hearing in the fog...An experiment

A Reminder

Part II: What Gets In The Way

Chapter Three: Exploring Beliefs...page 109

Growing into a healthy flower

1. Belief Work: Healing with Awareness...The heart attack...
Noticing and being curious too...Finding a new relationship with thought...
Family values

2. Going Deeper: Exploring blind spots...Hey you! Over here!...
Late for dinner...Some television history and more...
Loving enough to let others be...More about Naming Practice...
Helpful experiences and information

3. **Thoughts as visitors:** Focus and Awareness...
A lipstick story...Being aware and feeling at the same time...
No-thought experiences...It's up to us

Chapter Four: Fear as Fertilizer...page 139

Feel the fear and read this anyway

1. **Everyday Fear:** What is this, really?...A lost child...
   <u>F</u>alse <u>E</u>vidence <u>A</u>ppearing <u>R</u>eal...

2. **Learning from Fear:** Feeling and not reacting...
   Fears make us Stop, Look, and Listen...A personal example...
   A frightful hike...When dying is *what is*...
   Fears help wake us up

Chapter Five: Urban Meditator Devours Crocodile and Other Mistaken Ideas About Meditation...page 153

Top 12 Myths

Myth 1: Busy Myth
Different thought experiences

Myth 2: Control Myth

Myth 3: Sitting Still Myth

Myth 4: Must Be Comfortable Myth

Myth 5: Lotus Myth

Myth 6: Monk (Nun) Myth

Jennifer and Maddy

Myth 7: Time Myth

Myth 8: Other People Myth

Myth 9: Space Myth

Myth 10: Religious Myth

Myth 11: Study Myth

Myth 12: Can't Myth

A moment of reflection

Part III: Remembering Who We Really Are

Chapter Six: Beginning the Journey...page 177

Awareness: Noticing *what is*...Noticing thought, clouds moving...
Different tools of Awareness practice...
Practicing means practicing with Compassion

A natural evolution

Chapter Seven: Awareness and Meditation...page 183

1. Taking Five Minutes: After sitting...In the beginning

2. Practical Guidance: Breath practice...Whole body listening...
Pain in meditation...

3. A Few Words about Teachers: The stuff in the attic...
Noticing guidance ...We need to keep going

Part IV: The Adventure

Chapter Eight: Being Open With All of It...page 199

Gayle's story: Why people meditate...A fresh perspective...
Wanting to be helpful...Working with change...Being flexible...
Gayle's adventure begins...The real adventure

       Author's Note...page I
       Acknowledgments...page III
       Illustrations and Quote...page VII
       A Short List of Related Reading...page VIII
       CDs by Padme Nina Livingstone...page IX

Preface

What do we really want?

It's been said that the purpose of life is to find happiness. The word "happy" may be freely exchanged with love or joy. Isn't it true we all want to be happy? Don't we want to feel loved and to be loving and joyful?

Isn't it also true, much of the time, we are confused about how to be happy? We try all kinds of ways. We go to college with the dream of finding happiness in our chosen field. We get married thinking the other person will make us happy. We lose or gain weight, thinking our new body shape will make us happy. We buy a new car thinking that the car will make us happy.

Many of the things we desire, even hunger for—our material, sensual, or social goals—get us into trouble because of our attachment to the immediate pleasure they provide, or our ideas of the enduring pleasure we imagine they will give us at some time in the future. It can feel wonderful enjoying the immediate satisfaction of these kinds of desires, like a promotion, sexual intimacy, or a new home. However, the confusion arises when we mistakenly believe that these pleasurable experiences should continue, will be deeply fulfilling, and ensure long-lasting happiness. As our understanding of life deepens, we discover that our hunger for more money, more friends, and more stuff, leads us to perpetual dissatisfaction. We must be willing to look deeper within if we are going to find true happiness.

Looking within is not easy, though; we are often afraid of unexplored aspects of our self. We prefer the continual distraction from our pain and confusion that our habits, and our culture, readily provide. We like the comfortable feeling of sameness; we may even prefer our illusion of sameness and try to avoid change. But change happens. It is inevitable. Have you ever noticed how you want to be both happy and avoid change? Does it work? Without inner exploration, we continue to live confused, distracted lives.

Seeking happiness, avoiding pain

In our human condition, each one of us seeks happiness and avoids pain. We are built that way. It is just the way it is. Unless we develop our capabilities for knowing what's true, we continue to be confused about what brings us happiness. We also continue to be disappointed and in unnecessary pain.

Let's Not Call It Meditation looks at what gets in the way of who we long to be, so we can clear up our confusion about where to find happiness. Personal stories are shared which mirror the challenges we all face in life. Using the image of The Flowering of Inner Growth, we see how our deepest desires for a balanced, loving, and an essentially rewarding life are reflected in the beauty of a flower. Intention, our heart's longing, and energy are underpinnings of our development. Taking 100% responsibility for our actions, we explore aspects of our life with curiosity, humor, gratitude, compassion, and creativity.

We explore what gets in the way of clarity. We take a look at the role of "fear" and pain-producing beliefs in perpetuating our confusion. We show how confusion is created and how we can untangle it. We explore being still, focusing in the moment, and listening with openness to our body/mind[1] experience.

By practicing focusing within, we learn to honestly assess what will bring us true happiness. This does not mean we eliminate existing sources of satisfaction, pleasure, or fun. It means we are more honest, compassionate, and clear in each moment. We are present with joy, as well as sorrow. We are alive! Truly alive!

Patti's story

The guidance session was nearly over. Parked near the canal, we sat in the car. It was our first time together and Patti had told me her story. I had mentioned it was time to teach her a simple beginner's meditation.

"I don't meditate. It's not me," Patti exclaimed.

Honoring her resistance, I said, "Let's not call it meditation. Let me teach you a tool that will help you relax and learn how to focus your attention better."

She visibly relaxed. After a brief instruction on counting the breath, we sat still and silent for about three minutes.

Afterwards, Patti was smiling and said she had liked it and wanted to meet again.

What's in a word?

The word meditation has become mainstream, and it seems every person who has heard about meditation thinks of it differently. We have hopes about

---

[1] Body/mind is a term used to include all that occurs within the physical body and the mind. It points to the intimate connection between our response to thought and the physical and emotional sensations in the body.

Preface

the potential of meditation, and ingrained misconceptions about it too. "Nope. Not me. I could never sit still for an hour" and "It is something Buddhists do." Or "Wonderful, happy, special people meditate, not me." "The Dalai Lama meditates… but I can't get my thoughts to stop."

Meditation is used by most Eastern spiritual traditions to describe practices that help develop clarity, compassion, and awareness. In Western culture, it is often used to describe relaxation and self-hypnosis techniques, awareness practices, and visualization exercises for healing.

In the spring of 2003, I attended a health fair as a vendor. Many people attended a meditation session lead by a Qi Gong[2] therapist, and others attended a meditation session with a Kundalini yoga teacher. By the time they got to my table, I noticed each person thought of their own experience and assumed they knew all about meditation. The different uses of the word "meditation" can create confusion.

Patti was open to dropping the word "meditation." She had so many ideas about meditation; she would not even try it. It was helpful for Patti to stop using the word and not name the experience at all. The openness created by dropping a word which held so much meaning for her, was crucial to experiencing her inner silence with awareness. In fact, one way to describe meditation is "practicing awareness." It is a way of discovery, an adventurous journey through personal experience into what the Persian mystic Rumi called "the Sanctuary within."

---

[2] Qi Gong (pronounced chee gong) is an ancient Chinese energy healing practice.

Preface

Awareness is being open with *what is*. Awareness is also a word for feeling awake on all levels; physically, mentally, emotionally, and spiritually. Awake is when we get up in the morning with a clear mind and feel ready for whatever the day has in store. Our eyes, ears and senses are wide open. We notice details of how we are feeling, how clear the sky, or how defined each snowflake. We experience the smiles of others, and the humor in situations with a compassionate heart. Clarity, honesty, compassion, and gratitude are available when we are awake.

Yet, often we feel lost in "cloudy-brain" and experience resistance to our day. Thoughts come and go about all we have to do. We feel stressed even before we get out of bed. This cloudiness is sleepwalking in a state of mild to extreme confusion. It is maintained by our pushing against *what is*, instead of bringing curiosity to our situation, and waking up.

Wanting it to be easy

A seventy-year old woman, Ruth, came to me for guidance. At the end of our session, she wished out loud for a pill for more awareness. We burst out laughing. We laughed at the human condition that desires pills for everything. She laughed, too, at her sense of embarrassment to have said something "silly." I looked into her eyes, and realized she meant it! She really wished for a pill. She realized practicing being aware takes energy and she had already talked herself out of doing it.

As you read, check into your own prejudices and ideas about meditation. If the word "meditation" is not used, is there more openness? Opening up to your

Preface

own curiosity, you may discover feeling intrigued. With curiosity aroused, you can continue this adventure and find out for your self what it is all about.

This work has no pill as a substitute for experience. There is no pill for feeling fully alive! It takes energy, focus, and enough healthy desire to nourish the motivation for change. Cultivating awareness can be hard work.

The good news is I've never heard of anyone who regretted one moment of more awareness. Practicing awareness is what makes a life truly worth living. It brings authentic, deep happiness to our days.

Part I

Remembering Who We Long To Be

"And nothing is in the way."

The Flowering of Inner Growth

- Gratitude
- Humor
- Compassion for self and others
- 100% Responsibility
- Curiosity
- Creativity
- **Balance**

Light of Awareness

Intention
Longing
Energy

Roots of confusion: Mistaken beliefs about ourselves and the way the world works, unconsciously nourished throughout our lives.

Seeds of experience

Chapter One
Seven Key Elements for Growth

The Flowering of Inner Growth

The flower picture offers a way to visualize our innate potential to blossom. The Flowering of Inner Growth (see illustration at the beginning of Part I) represents the flowering of our spiritual, mental, emotional, and physical being. When we are awake, we are blossoming. As we study the flower, we are reminded of our potential. It serves as a visual reminder of what we embody when we are being who we long to be.[3]

All parts of the developing flower are interconnected and interdependent. Overdeveloping or ignoring any aspect puts the system out of Balance[4] and creates a form of dis-ease. Coming into Balance is a continual process. We flourish whenever we bring our attention to whoever (or whatever) is present.

Our Intention to blossom is kept alive by our heart's Longing for more love and joy in our life. Energy feeds the process of growth; the way flowers need the Energy of the sun to prosper. The roots of our plant go deep into our history and develop from our seed experiences.

Just as the light of the sun brings life to all that grows, the Light of Awareness brings life to our hearts and minds as we learn to be with *what is*. Awareness helps us integrate new perspectives about what is real and what is

---

[3] The words "being who we long to be" are meant as a pointer to our longing for wholeness. With Awareness, we experience our wholeness and there is no "longing" for anything else. We are present with all that *is*.

[4] For the remainder of the book, the seven key elements, Intention, Longing, Energy, Roots of Confusion, Desire for Change, Light of Awareness, and Balance, on the illustration will be capitalized to remind the reader of The Flowering of Inner Growth.

not. And the Desire to Change activates our growth. Fueled by a deep Longing, awakening Energy, Intention, and Awareness, it works through us to bring our life into Balance, the natural expression of our Being.

The flower is a perfect image for our being because flowers grow from seeds, just as we do. Flowers have all they need to break through the earth's crust into the light of day. We also have exactly what we need to break through our fearful, confused ways of being, and emerge into the light of day.

Awareness *is* our light of day. The capacity to be aware provides us with heart-healing gifts of presence, clarity, and Compassion, and we cultivate our own unique expression of the human condition as these qualities blossom within us.

The flower blooms with the Light of Awareness in this moment. We are awake. And nothing is in the way. Trying to explain this is like trying to describe the fragrance of a lilac to someone who has never smelled one— but experience one whiff, and…

1. Intention

Did you ever notice how easy it is on New Year's Eve to resolve to change unhealthy behavior and how hard it is to do it? It has become humorous to hear about New Year's resolutions because so few of us follow through on our aspirations. That is the difference between New Year's resolutions, or simple Intentions, and *activated* good Intentions. New Year's resolutions, simple Intentions, and activated good Intentions come from the same place—our pain and suffering.[5] You know when you are doing something that feels harmful—too much working, arguing, complaining, smoking, drinking, holiday eating, or playing. You vow to do better and find a Balance in the coming year. And then there is a birthday party the following weekend and beautiful desserts…and…oh, well, there is always next week, next month, next year!

Activated good Intentions are essential for growth because they move us towards healthy change. Resolutions are ideas that sound and feel good, yet we aren't necessarily willing to do the work to follow through. We formulate good Intentions, and forget them just as readily. Then, something mysterious happens. With a moment of Awareness, something inexplicable can shift. There can be a meaningful Desire for Change where there wasn't before and our good Intention becomes *activated*.

Everyone has a different threshold for what that something might be. Some people might swear off excessive drinking a hundred times before they decide that they've really had enough. Other people take one drink too much one time, and never drink too much alcohol again. It is like that with all kinds of habitual, pain-producing behaviors. One moment our habit owns us, and the next moment there is Awareness and clarity, and an important shift begins.

The opportunity to witness our life differently comes with a moment of Awareness. There is no telling when we will have had *enough* and be ready for real

---

[5] The initial pain we experience from the loss of a loved one, losing a job, or realizing one has a chronic illness is natural. Yet when we experience continual suffering from these events, it is our unconscious beliefs ("This shouldn't happen," "It's not fair," " It's too much, etc.") about these experiences that change the initial pain into suffering.

change. Yet, it is only at that point of *enough* that activated good Intentions can come alive. Until that moment, we are blind to our habits.

We usually go back and forth, remembering and forgetting, as Awareness brings us closer and closer to an activated Intention to change. Our activated good Intentions stay alive when we have experienced enough pain from what hasn't worked so far. At that moment, we are willing to do whatever it takes— for as long as it takes— to change our behavior.

Activated good Intentions are directly linked to a healthy desire to change unhealthy behaviors. The words themselves can help us remember this. Have you ever used the spelling of words to playfully trigger new meaning? By playing a bit with the words *Intention* and *behavior*, phrases emerge that can help us remember how the words are linked on a deep level.

Reading the word Intention, we can find *ten*ding to our *in*ner life. We tend to our inner life when we stop to smell the flowers or offer a hug to a friend in need. We tend to our inner life, by bringing curiosity and loving Awareness to our present experience, whether it is pleasant or unpleasant. Similarly, we can see the words *be* and *hav*e in the word behavior. A playful connection might suggest that our behavior displays how we are *be*ing with what we *have*, like kindness and patience or anger and impatience.

Any good Intention starts with a thought. The thought might be, "I want to develop more Compassion" or "I want to be nicer to my parents." The thought might be an open question like, "Who am I?" An activated good Intention is when we take a thought and work with it, bringing it to life. Thus, activated good Intentions (*inner tending*) lead to changes in our behavior (*being-with-what-we-have*).

Remembering Who We Long To Be

Holding an Intention for self-growth is a kind of goal-less goal. We rarely win a prize for pursuing this kind of goal. We can't know how things will turn out as we move through life with this Intention. We simply focus more often on our inner life, practice being mindful, and work on changing our behavior. We see the results over time, much like tending a garden.

Activated good Intentions have a powerful effect on our actions and the way we treat our self and others. An activated New Years resolution to stop smoking means we follow through until we find what works for us to stop smoking. Holding an Intention to become more compassionate, may lead us to work at a homeless shelter or a prison. Holding an Intention to be more patient with our children, might lead us to a meditation class, psychotherapy, a parenting skills workshop, or a recommended book. Holding an Intention to find an answer to the question, "Who am I?" might lead us to seeking guidance from a meditation teacher. Living from activated good Intentions, we learn to be more patient, thoughtful, and present with *what is*.

Intention is the heart and mental strength we bring to the process of waking up, or blossoming. Just as it takes hard, sustained effort to make strong muscles, it takes hard work to activate our Intentions. Just as flowers need their full season to bloom, it takes work and time to be the person we long to be.

The petals of our "flower" open as we experience our life through clear, loving, activated Intention. When our heart and mind are connected, and our Intentions and actions are aligned, we open the gateway to our flowering potential..

A love triangle

Here's a story about how activating good Intentions for growth changed the behavior of a woman caught up in a messy situation with her best friend and her husband. Joan came for guidance because she was intensely stressed, and uncomfortable enough to want to change her behavior. Her best friend, Carol, and her husband, Jack, had been emotionally intimate without telling her. She had found out about their daily contact, intimate conversations, and lunch dates, and let them know how she felt. Carol and Jack had stopped seeing each other and Joan cut off relations with Carol. Yet, now Joan was obsessively checking her husband's things for signs of his going back on his word. Jack felt invaded, and furious, as Joan ignored his boundaries again and again. Their marriage was in trouble and she knew it.

Joan realized she was damaging their relationship with her untrusting, invasive behavior. She didn't understand what was causing her compulsion to go through Jack's stuff, but she intended to stop before she destroyed what was left of their marriage. Joan wanted to heal the pain she was feeling. She thought this meant she needed to first forgive Jack. Joan emailed me that she had a "forgiveness issue" and wanted to meet.

As Joan shared her story, it became clear to me that there was a mistaken belief behind Joan's fury and feelings of betrayal. I asked Joan to reflect honestly about with whom she was most angry. After a brief moment, she realized, to her surprise, she felt more anger towards Carol than her husband. We then focused on exploring the belief underneath her anger towards her friend.

Remembering Who We Long To Be

It didn't take Joan long to realize that she felt betrayed. She had a belief: Women should never betray a woman friend for a man. Joan's belief made her feel betrayed and furious. When Joan explored whether the belief was true or false, she felt confused about her unquestioned belief, which she assumed was true. Confusion always arises when a belief about the world comes into conflict with the way things *are*.

Carol did what Joan believed no woman friend should do. With careful, thoughtful exploration, it became glaringly clear to Joan that her fundamental belief was based on fiction about how she thought life *should* be, not the way things *are*.

Once Joan experienced *what is*, rather than how she thought things should be, she discovered another unexplored belief at the root of her angry and confused feelings towards Jack. "Husbands should never become intimate with other women." This also created confusion for Joan, because in reality Jack did become emotionally intimate with another woman.

Joan easily made the connection between her two mistaken[6] beliefs and felt relieved by what felt more true to her. Joan felt Carol was ignoring their friendship when she spent time developing an intimate relationship with Jack. And Jack explored an intimate friendship with his wife's best friend behind her back. Fighting what had really happened caused Joan tremendous confusion and pain.

Let's set aside the moral discussion about whether Jack and Carol's behavior was right or wrong. Joan uncovered two beliefs that were based on

---

[6] Suggestion: Check within to feel your response to the word "mistaken." Do you experience it as a judgment? It is not meant to be. Can you see that the word "mistaken" need not be judgmental? It is simply a part of the learning process we all experience when we make mistakes, gain insight, and keep going.

assumptions about how she felt things should be. Our assumptions cause pain when they conflict with the way things are. Joan still had strong feelings that needed exploration, yet she reported feeling a sense of freedom and ease. The truth was strong medicine, and provided a sense of relief, like a splash of cold water on a hot day.

Joan's initial Intention to forgive Jack had brought her to guidance. Her desire to feel better and change compulsive, invasive behavior fueled her exploration with me. Her willingness to examine her mistaken beliefs allowed an open exploration to uncover what felt more true to her.

Joan observed that part of her anger was based on assumptions she could now see through. She realized the most immediate issue had been untangling confusion between her attachments to two beliefs and what had actually happened, rather than forgiveness. As soon as the truth was seen, her attachments to those two mistaken beliefs vanished and she felt better. She left our session with a more honest, compassionate perspective. Joan was able to go home to a husband who had made a commitment to their relationship when he stopped seeing Carol. Joan could enjoy that relationship if she continued to explore what is true, as thoughts arise about the past. There are probably other beliefs about marriage and relationship that will need to be explored as time goes on. Joan's experience was likely just the beginning of discovering how to live with a new perspective.

What happened to the issue of forgiveness? Blaming creates the need for forgiveness. Thoughts that create blame need to be explored completely. Joan was caught up in blaming Carol and Jack for doing something she felt was wrong, as well as feeling they did something wrong to her, making her feel like a victim to their actions. Her understanding had transformed two beliefs, but as long as she continued to blame them in any way, she would continue to feel like a victim. Also, Joan would likely need to forgive herself for her behavior with her husband's belongings. As long as we blame, there is a need to feel forgiveness, for our self and others.

As every mistaken belief that creates blaming is understood and transformed, our heart is also transformed. As long as Joan keeps her Intention to find out what's true, she holds the possibility of seeing through every mistaken belief that has kept her angry and hurting. If she does her work, the whole issue of forgiveness will fall away, and leave Awareness and Compassion in its place. When Joan stops blaming her husband, her friend, and herself, she will be free of having to forgive anyone in this messy situation. She will be free to notice what's happening right in front of her, without anything from the past getting in the way.

Good Intentions help develop discretion

Discretion is a gift that comes with Awareness. With the Intention to be Compassionate, responsible, and aware, a connection can be made between our impulse to do something and our understanding of a possible result. With Awareness, we move towards more loving behavior and leave less loving action alone. Our Intentions become healthier and more focused with discretion.

Discretion is an essential ingredient in activated good Intentions. Discretion is when we pause before we speak or act, and have a sense of the bigger picture.

Discretion is a union among our Intention, our understanding, and our actions. We employ discretion when we decide to hold our tongue and not tell a friend when we think they look awful. Instead, we ask how they are feeling. With discretion, we use kind words and leave unkind words alone.

Indiscretion is like walking around with a blindfold on, blind to the consequences of our behavior. Joan had no discretion when she rampaged through her husband's stuff. Most of us know people (including one's self) who at times act in ways that demonstrate their lack of Awareness about the consequences of their behavior.

Learning the hard way

A while ago, our son, Jason, turned seventeen. Two days after his birthday, Jason went to a concert and accepted a couple of alcoholic drinks. After the concert, he and his friends got into his car and headed home. On the way, a police officer noticed the brake light was out and pulled them over. Jason failed the sobriety tests. He was arrested and taken to the police station in handcuffs.

Jason had to deal with the consequences; a possible DWI, and the court system. He lost his driving privileges. He also lost his chance to play in sectional soccer games for his high school. Obviously, he was not using good discretion that night. It was a blessing no one was hurt.

The day after his arrest, Jason said to me, "I guess I wasn't ready to drive." Jason wanted me to use his story in this book. He planned to join a school club called SADD (Students Against Destructive Decisions), and hoped to help others make smart decisions. His ability to use discretion the next time improved with his experience and understanding.

Jason is learning discretion. As well as having the Intention to not hurt others, we also need to use our mental abilities too. We need to remember that drinking and driving is extremely dangerous for everybody. Then, we can think before we act. We can say, "No thank you" when offered alcohol and want to drive. We can also say, "No thank you" to drugs or other experiences, which can be self-destructive, or harmful to others.

What was our reaction to the whole mess Jason created? Naturally, we were concerned about the possibility of him having hurt someone or himself because of his lack of discretion, yet we listened to his story with Awareness, without blame and anger. On reflection, we realized that our years of meditation came to good use. We noticed what needed to be done: take away driving privileges, call the school athletic director, and call a lawyer.

My Awareness practice was especially useful the week before we went to court. I was caught up in fear over not having any control over what the courts might do to Jason. As I let myself get carried away, I felt upset and afraid for my son. The body[7] reacted from my fears, and I developed an upset stomach, headaches, and nausea. Paying attention to my feelings, I remembered the practice of Wanting Nothing.

---

[7] Using *the* body, rather than *my* body, is a way of describing the physical body in a simple way, without the unnecessary addition of an "I" who owns it.

Wanting nothing

Allowing myself to get caught up in wanting to control another person, or the results of a situation that I can't control— I've learned to drop the wanting, and want nothing. This does not mean I'm passive and turn off my feelings or actions. In fact, it means I stay awake and open, so I can notice *what is* and respond with Awareness, clarity, and Compassion to whatever is happening.

I've often been asked whether it is really possible to "want nothing." Isn't it true we have natural desires for love, food, comfort, and good health? Yes, this is part of the human condition. In addition, it is healthy and natural to want other people to treat us with respect and unconditional love.

As a person expresses anger towards us with unkind words, we certainly may experience hurt feelings. Having a thought of wanting someone to be different makes sense when we feel hurt from what was said or done to us. The problems arise every time we go from simply wanting to be treated with kindness to *habitually* wanting people and things to be different than they are. Believing our thoughts that things should be different, our "wanting" gets the better of us. We are struggling against *what is*. This struggle adds more pain to the initial pain we experienced.

Yet, being fully with uncomfortable feelings, without pulling away, we can discover what happens as we allow our feelings to run through us without getting caught up in them. Wanting nothing from the angry person, we may recover easily, and realize the other person was having a bad moment. We may have nothing to say, we may walk away, or stay and say something helpful. Then, we haven't let our uncomfortable experience ruin our day or our relationship.

It is just like having a stress headache. It hurts. Now imagine continually fighting it and trying to push it away. Our whole body/mind system tightens in the ensuing battle. Most of us realize this battling doesn't work. We may even understand that it can make the headache feel worse. It is the same with beliefs. Unless we bring Awareness to our situation, and drop the wanting people to be different, we feed the pain, and remain confused about what happened. Wanting nothing, infused with Awareness, lightens our view so that we can be with *what is*.

Feeling open to everything

Wanting to change people and things we cannot change continually creates havoc in relationships—like spending time with family members who don't behave the way we wish. Or, finding ourselves involved with the court system because of something someone else has done. We can drop our attachment to how it all turns out, and be open to the experience, as it unfolds. It's not always easy to do, but being open to the experience can feel much better, as the following examples demonstrate.

My practice of Wanting Nothing began a few years ago on a family car trip to visit my in-laws on Cape Cod. It had been several years since we were there, and even though I love the Cape, all I felt was dread. It was difficult for my mother-in-law to share her kitchen space, yet we needed certain food because of dietary needs. In the past, I would arrive with our assorted staples, put them in a corner of the kitchen counter and she would stay out of the kitchen as much as possible. I had the sense that as soon as we arrived, my father-in-law took over cooking because she couldn't bear having her kitchen space disrupted.

This time as we drove over the bridge onto the Cape, two words appeared in my mind, "Want nothing." "Hmm," I thought, "that's interesting." The words repeated several times. I had these word experiences before, and although I don't know their origin, I always sense their truth.

I reflected on the meaning of the words and realized how much I wanted my in-laws to be different. I noticed I wanted a lot from them. I wanted to be asked about my life. I wanted them to care about me and show it in the way I would choose.

"Want nothing? Hmmmm." I realized they didn't give me what I wanted. In fact, the more I wanted them to behave in particular ways, the unhappier I became. They didn't notice anything amiss, while I just got more and more unhappy and withdrawn.

Here was another possibility. Want nothing. A fresh, new Intention opened up like the first sight of clear, blue, ocean on the side of the road. I decided to notice when I wanted anything from them and not feed the feeling of wanting them to be different. It worked!

The Awareness I brought to "wanting nothing" began to dissolve much of my resistance before we even arrived. It was the first of many lovely visits. I still need to enter the mode of "Not Wanting" before we visit them. Our foods are still different, but our presence is welcomed, even in the kitchen. I know I'll be mostly listening when we visit, because that is what they want, and that is enough.

Wanting nothing, I am open to *what is*, and I receive all that is, as it is! I feel open to everything!

With Jason's drinking/driving mistake and the court process, *wanting nothing* meant that although I would do everything I could to help effect a good court decision, I had to drop my fears about what the judge would decide. I left the judging to the judge. It also meant I had to drop my expectations as they arose about how Jason would handle his consequences. Then, I could experience the freedom to be with *what is*, instead of how I wanted it to be. I knew Jason would be capable of handling what he had created. He was learning discretion. He was also learning Responsibility for his actions. Our job as parents has been to help him grow by staying open, and responding to him with love and clarity, one moment at a time.

Is it possible to want nothing from others? It depends on your Intention. From my experience, *not wanting* is possible—and it is a moment-to-moment practice. Wanting Nothing practice feeds an entirely different kind of wanting than the kind that creates confusion. This vastly different kind of wanting can be called longing.

In standard usage, we often find the two words *wanting* and *longing* used interchangeably. Here, the two words are being used in distinctly different ways. Wanting comes from the mind that is never satisfied, always feels incomplete, and is attached to the notion of individuality—causing us to feel separate from other people and the natural world. Longing, on the other hand, comes from the heart, and expresses our intrinsic desire to move towards wholeness. Longing allows us to experience our connection with other people and our natural world. Longing brings openness, light, and love, instead of tightness, confusion, and fear. It expresses our desire for experiencing long-lasting happiness.

2. Longing

The heart's Longing for wholeness is what brings the people in my vision to the shore of the lake. This Longing is part of our spiritual nature. The people on the shore feel *enough* connected with their Longing, to stay and satisfy their Curiosity. People who aren't ready walk away from the lake. They may follow others for a while, but they won't stay at the lake. Their Longing is still asleep. Their curiosity about exploring new possibilities for a richer life has not been aroused.

Our heart's Longing is essential food for our growing plant. Of course, flowers don't long for anything. They grow, blossom, and die. Nothing more. They do not have mistaken beliefs, which get in the way of experiencing their intrinsic wholeness. Flowers do not experience confusion and do not have to surrender to something beyond their understanding. In fact, flowers point to the simplicity of our being *enough*, just as we *are*. The deeper we connect with our heart's Longing, the simpler it is to keep questioning our pain-producing beliefs. And the simpler it is to remember that this is the journey we want to consciously embrace. The heart's Longing is the desire for Awareness and love.

How does our Longing fit into cultivating Awareness? First, the mind must be open at least a crack to notice the heart's Longing. Although this Longing is always available, we can be completely closed off from it. Our eyes must be open at least a little bit. Understanding the *possibility* that we can live with less suffering and confusion means understanding that the potential for healthy change is always present. Once we understand and move towards embracing change, we can develop the skills necessary for the journey. Then we can welcome Longing into our life, and open the way for our deepest healing.

Usually, our experiences of Longing come and go unrecognized. We hear an inspiring story or beautiful words, feel better for a while, and then return to the *status quo*. Reading a self-help article may give us a temporary inkling of our possibility for change. As that inkling becomes stronger, and we stay open, Curiosity may be aroused. Activated Curiosity about our present condition becomes the natural expression of our Longing for wholeness. Then our Curiosity can bring a gentle questioning into our painful situation and the possibility for healing.

Our Longing for deep healing is an essential aspect of being human. It helps us remember the path to inner growth is right in front of us, even as we experience forgetfulness and painful times. We find the strength to go on with the work—practicing being aware, even with our pain. Through our Longing, we begin to heal, and glimpse a life of wholeness, of integrity.

As our Balance is disturbed less and less by chaotic circumstances, our behavior displays our clarity and natural equanimity. We know for our self what is true, as we live with more Balance, feeling well-grounded in the full integration of our experience and understanding.

A personal story

The beginning of my meditation practice was completely rooted in Longing. In my mid-twenty's I began to make connections between difficulties I was having in my relationships with other people, and not feeling loved and loving. I longed to feel loved, and to be loving.

When I first began to meditate in 1976, I had excellent guidance from Roshi Philip Kapleau and Toni Packer at the Rochester Zen Center. I felt the rightness of the path, and continued going to meditation sittings out of a deep desire to stop my pain. I had faith in every word I heard about the eventual benefits from this meditation work and longed to experience those benefits first hand. I felt connected to, and grateful for, all the people who had gone before me.

For the first two years in Rochester, my husband-to-be Bill and I attended every possible sitting and talk at the Zen Center. We were hungry for more clarity and dedicated our lives to finding it. Longing is what got us out of bed for the early morning sittings every weekday. Longing is what got us to every two-and-a-half hour evening sitting. Longing got us to attend our first all-day sitting and then, the silent meditation retreats we have attended since then.

Especially in the beginning of inner growth work and meditation, Longing keeps us going. Some people feel benefits right away. However, it takes a while for some of us to feel the benefits in our daily life. We may meet others who inspire us with their behavior, and may hear inspiring stories. So, we keep going, and after awhile, we begin to notice changes. We may have more patience with our children, or take a moment to consider the consequences before blurting out a critical comment to our spouse. We may even witness family members or co-workers changing because we've changed. We may experience a heightened sense of being alive and happy.

Jackie's story

When I first began teaching meditation, I worked with a woman named Jackie, who said she longed for clarity and was new to meditating. I suggested to Jackie that she practice saying, "I am" to herself, with each out breath.[8] Jackie worked with "I am" for a week and was strongly upset by her experience. Each time she said, "I am" her mind filled in the sentence with words like lazy, too slow, ugly, not good enough, and so on. She felt terrible and didn't know what to do with all the negative stuff.

I had imagined something quite different. Clearly, my instructions were incomplete. I was new and had much to learn. Jackie was very unhappy and I was so startled at what came up for her, and limited in my own understanding at the time, I didn't have useful guidance for her. Without proper guidance, Jackie stopped coming. I hope her Longing brought her a better teacher than I was at the time. I've often wished I could talk with her again.

Today, I would tell Jackie to listen with full attention to the mind that completes the sentence in a negative. Believing untrue thoughts, like mistaken beliefs about the self, literally causes the Energy to get stuck somewhere in the

---

[8] "I am" is actually the only completely truthful words we can ever say about who we are, because it includes all of our physical, mental, emotional, and spiritual reality in the moment. Anything else we say is only a part of the truth, as "I am breathing" doesn't include the reality that I am also hearing, or seeing, or talking. When we simply say, "I am", without adding anything, just as it is, "I am" can bring us directly into the moment. All thoughts of worry, anger, frustration, judgment and blame can fall away. Some people say, "I am" to help focus their Awareness practice. Others use "I am" as their only practice.

body. I would suggest Jackie notice how the body responds to negative words; what does the body feel like when negative self-talk is going on? Is there a tightening, any discomfort?

We can Stop, Look, and Listen when it's important, just as we learned when we were young. The body is our natural Stop sign whenever we believe judgmental thoughts, like I am lazy, slow, ugly, etc. Experiencing discomfort, we can Stop what we're doing and bring our attention to it. We can Look within, and notice where the discomfort is and how it feels. And we can Listen to "hear" if there is a message for us.

There is a continual interplay between our curiosity about the cause of our discomfort—like the uncomfortable sensations one feels when caught up in blame, and self-judgment— and simply being aware, being with *what is*. Jackie would need to *wonder* if her beliefs behind the words are true or not. Questioning is wonderful because Curiosity about negative self-talk literally transforms it.

Open questioning, without expectations or conditions, creates a healthy distance[9] from our uncomfortable feelings. We "step back" a bit from our discomfort as we question what is happening, not knowing what the result will be. Questioning like this, we are children again, playing in the earth, looking for hidden treasure, happy with anything we find.

---

[9] A healthy distance is created when we uncritically witness our sensations (and thoughts). We are able to simply observe what is happening within, no longer caught up in wanting it to be different. The part of us that unconditionally witnesses is not the same as the part that is caught up in reaction. We are watching the internal "movie" of our feelings. The feeling or sensation, just like watching a TV movie, is just *what is*.

Then we can explore, without fear, any dark feelings these thoughts create. Once pain-producing mistaken beliefs are brought to light, and seen as untrue, they dissolve. At root, Awareness and meditation are about finding out what is true and what is not. To find out what is true, we cultivate a questioning mind, and question thoughts that create painful experiences. I hope Jackie found the freedom she longed for, by exploring her pain-producing thoughts to discover what they were— simply not true.

Our Longing changes over time. Wondering about our pain-producing thoughts allows what's true to be seen and what's not true to fall away. We stop taking other people's unkind behavior personally. The heart feels full. Noticing our life unfold, we are more firmly rooted in *what is*, and spiritual Longing is such a part of our life that we no longer need to remember or forget it. We are who we longed to be. Our Longing is embraced in Awareness. And we move through life with more Compassion, clarity, and presence.

3. Energy

Energy is an essential element of all life. Energy *is* life. We *are* Energy. The Flower of Inner Growth represents our deepest healing. Interestingly, the word healing is derived from "haelen," the Greek word for "to be whole." It is important to do what we can to keep our Energy balanced—the life blood of our mental, physical, emotional, and spiritual being—because we want to feel whole, and heal deeply.

Eastern medicine helps us understand about Energy, and that it is important to keep it Balanced and flowing as freely as possible. The relationship between flowing, or unblocked Energy, and healing, is an integral part of all Eastern medicine practices. The quality and quantity of our Energy flow is influenced by the internal condition of our mental, emotional, physical, and spiritual being as well as our interaction with our environment. There are too many factors affecting our Energy flow to mention here. What's important is to understand that when we don't feel well it means our Energy is out-of-balance. Our Energy system needs help returning to its natural Balance when this happens.

Shifting attitude, shifting Energy

Negative mind states create and aggravate problems in the body. The Energy system reflects our confusion. We can feel tired, and even exhausted, from negative self-talk. Energy is generated by the active exploration of negative mind states. Rather than staying stuck with thinking "Life is happening to me and I can't do anything about it," or "I can't handle this," we can move to "I'm okay" and "I can handle this."

Awareness naturally shifts our actions and attitudes, and we feel more alive. We all tend to move in and out of the victim mind state. Touching it again, like touching a hot stove, reminds us that feeding the Poor Me mind state is unloving. Eventually, being more loving with our self, we live completely free of feeling like a victim.

Our attitudes greatly influence our daily life, even as we deal with difficult health issues. For example, my client Alex, had been struggling with a Poor Me attitude and low Energy, and was beginning to get unstuck from it. Alex was a 28-year old man with fibromyalgia, chronic fatigue, terrible headaches, mental illness, back troubles, sleep problems, rashes, and food and medicine allergies. He was on welfare and had never been physically or mentally stable enough to receive training or hold a job. Alex had a different doctor for each symptom and none of them spoke to each other. He wanted to feel better and had been meeting with me for guidance for several months. We met at a diner across from his apartment building in the city.

Alex had felt like a victim to the pain and dis-ease in his body and mind for his entire life. He had been to psychiatrists, psychotherapists, and doctors since childhood, and his troubles continued. A part of Alex believed that nothing more could be done to explore his mental and physical problems. Before our work together, he felt hopeless and trapped by a mind and body he called "beyond help!"

One day during a guidance session, I realized that Alex might be gluten intolerant. I had recently seen a list of the varied and apparently disconnected symptoms that can result from a lifetime of consuming foods with wheat because the body has an allergy or intolerance to gluten. All of Alex's physical and mental problems were on the list of symptoms of gluten intolerance.

I told Alex what I had learned about gluten intolerance. As we realized the possibilities, we shared tears, and laughter. As an experiment, Alex decided he had to stop eating any foods containing gluten for two weeks to find out if gluten was a likely cause of his symptoms.

Alex went shopping and bought a couple of week's worth of gluten free food with his food stamps. The food lasted three weeks and he felt much better all around. He was sleeping better, peeing less frequently, had more Energy, less pain, better memory, and his thinking had more clarity. He felt there was a clear connection between eating gluten and many of his difficulties.

Alex's attitude about his problems shifted. He had Energy to make changes. He realized the next step was to get a doctor's diagnosis. He needed to get more food stamp money to purchase more expensive gluten-free food. He needed a medical prescription for nutritional support to help the body/mind heal from years of eating gluten.

Alex still got caught up in feeling like a victim. However, armed with new information and the extraordinary experience of feeling and sleeping better when he was off gluten, he was gaining the strength he needed. He went back to eating wheat, so his body could reflect the gluten intolerance for the medical tests he would have to undergo to confirm his condition for the medical and welfare establishment. He felt his symptoms return, but he was aware of the cause. Alex was making the connection between his diet and how he felt, and the victim feelings were less frequent. He remembered more often that he could take charge and find the difference between being happy or miserable. Maybe one day, Alex will wake up, and realize he is done with Poor Me for good.

Finding the Balance

Finding what is true and what is not true was part of Alex's process of learning and growth. The process would continue as he dealt with the health system and provided information to his doctors so they could connect the dots, and potentially confirm what he believed to be true. He felt he had been dealing with wheat allergy or gluten intolerance his whole life and was seeing light at the end of the tunnel. He had a whole lot more Energy for being alive!

Alex needed to continue his practice of Awareness, as he interacted with the health care system. Feeling angry or Poor Me got in the way of Alex's Energy. The body heard, "Poor Me" and responded with, "Oh, I am in bad shape!" The body responded as if the thought were true.

In fact, believing a negative thought affects the body/mind, and the body's Energy gets stuck. As a result, we can easily feel depleted. Feeling weaker, we tend to anger more easily, and our anger generally upsets the very people who can help us. And then we may think, "Nobody likes me" or "I'm not worthy" and feel even worse. These cycles continue until we become curious about what we can do differently, and make a change from within.

There is a time for receiving care and help from others. The practice of Awareness, which refines discernment, makes it easier to determine when we need help from family, friends, doctors, complementary health care providers, or teachers. Awareness helps us receive the help as a part of what we can do for our self. Dropping the Poor Me, and surrendering to *what is* works best.

Life works much better when we are clear and patient. Our thoughts may then sound like, "What can I do to help this difficult process?" or "Maybe this woman just needs me to smile at her" or "I am handling this." Our body's Energy flows better because we are flowing with *what is*. Then we have more Energy to deal with any challenging situation.

We need strong mental Energy to do the work of Awareness. In order to have strong mental Energy, it is important to do what we can to keep the body in good health. Body and mind are completely connected. Whenever possible, eat nutritional foods, take appropriate supplements, sleep well, enjoy regular exercise, and get appropriate professional assistance as needed. This can help keep the body/mind in Balance and our Energy flowing better. We also need to be curious about how negative mind states affect our situation.

Active Curiosity

Alex brought his curiosity to our guidance sessions each time we met. He knew that whatever he was doing wasn't working well enough to suit him, and was curious about the possibility of living with less emotional and physical pain. Even though he was often in great pain and weak from fatigue at the outset of our meeting times, Alex would leave energized, noticeably feeling better.[10]

People who bring curiosity to the way things *are*, change their relationship with the pain itself. Usually when we are in pain, we immediately want it to go away. This is natural. It may give us momentary relief to take a pill for our headache, turn on the television in the middle of an argument, or assign blame—to oneself or another person— for our pain. Yet, when we blame, push against pain, or ignore it, does it help in the long run?

It is curiosity that keeps us open to fresh perspectives and our potential for deep healing as we actively wonder about the cause of our pain and suffering.

---

[10] Alex has healed well enough to attend college. And at publishing time, he was getting excellent grades.

Questioning what's happening, remaining non-judgmental and unattached to a particular result, we are open to *what is*.

Have you noticed how often thoughts of your self and others are about right or wrong, good or bad, pass or fail? Allowing judgmental thoughts to pass through the mind, without getting caught up in them, we can be open and wonder about whether they are true. Then we can notice what's really happening when there is no judgment in the way.

Sometimes, we don't even realize we have judgments. As an experiment, try a practice suggested by Jack Kornfield,[11] a meditation teacher. Simply sit still and count judgmental thoughts for one hour. A thought like, "I don't like doing this." becomes Judgment Number One. Or "My knee hurts too much." becomes Judgment Number Two. "This feels stupid" becomes Judgment Number Three, and so on. Counting judgments helps us become more aware of what occupies our mind, especially as we notice the judgments of the judgments!

Actually, non-judgmental wondering about our inner life gives us Energy. There is less of a struggle. Our openness keeps the Energy from getting stuck. Sometimes pain lessens or vanishes completely when we are exploring it with open, active curiosity. We find it easier to be with situations the way they are, without the additional, unnecessary, and exhausting mental work of resisting *what is*. Our experience of life changes for the better.

---

[11] Kornfield, Jack, A Path with Heart, New York: Bantam Books, 1993

When pain is *all that is*

In the moments when seemingly unbearable physical or emotional pain is present, before a medicine takes effect, or before we can take action to change our situation, it is still possible to be with *what is*. Tension is created between what we want to be different, and what we cannot change. *What is* is pain and we naturally want it to stop. We think about wanting it to go away. Pushing against pain in the body makes the muscles tighten around the nerves and the struggle only makes the pain worse. Fighting pain requires our Energy and we tire from the struggle. Feeding the Poor Me drains us even more.

Curiosity allows us to explore *what is*, and allows us to stay with the pain sensations without making it worse. We can notice how the pain is nuanced. We can feel subtle changes in temperature, muscle tension, and how the sensations travel in the body.[12] We are fully with the pain, and we have more Energy in reserve because it is less of a battle to stay with *what is*. Awareness directly effects healing. It is the same way with emotional and spiritual pain. Our ability to be with the pain changes our experience of it. Bringing curiosity to our sensations, instead of trying to push them away, or ignore them, can lead to understanding, patience, and Energy, instead of denial, impatience, and resistance.

As we grow in Awareness, we learn how much the mind affects our pain. We learn that even naming sensations as "pain" makes it more challenging to be with *what is* because of all our associations and unconscious programming tied to the word. We can also use the mind to focus our attention on the breath when we

---

[12] Also, there are times when it is important and loving to take pain medication.

experience pain. Staying focused with the breath helps us be with the pain differently. We may notice its intensity diminish as we gently focus on the breath in the midst of our discomfort.

There certainly may be physical, social, and environmental causative factors to having pain and dis-ease. Yet we can still develop a healthy relationship with thoughts and body sensations. We can develop a sense of what is true, and practice being present with whatever is happening. Surrendering more easily to *what is*, allows space and Energy for exploration of what's true and what's more loving.

4. Roots of Confusion

Coming into this world, we are basically open and innocent, ready to receive all that life has to offer. Life offers us the seeds of experience, as depicted in The Flowering of Inner Growth. We make decisions about ourselves, and our world and the way it works, based on these seed experiences. We decide if we are lovable or not, based on how others treat us. We innocently decide whether the world is a safe place. We decide whether we are intelligent, attractive, funny, friendly, useful, clever, or belligerent, in large part from our interpretations of how others treat us. We continually and unconsciously build mistaken beliefs from our personal collection of "seeds of experience."

Another interesting thing happens. As we are growing up, we don't question these mistaken beliefs. We assume that what we believe is true and how the world works. We don't realize we can question our beliefs; we don't know it is good to question them. The media, our immediate and extended family, educational, religious and political institutions often reinforce our confusion. We may not even realize we *have* mistaken beliefs that relate to our identity and self-image.

For example, if there is a belief that "I am unworthy," there may be a tendency to not do well in the world. The assumption of failure is attached to this mistaken belief. Even when things are going well for us, we may sabotage ourselves because we unconsciously believe in our failure, so why bother?

Even though our beliefs can cause us emotional, mental, physical and spiritual suffering, we become "comfortable" with the pain because it is familiar. We need to be willing to explore being uncomfortable if we want to untangle our confusion and continue our healing process.

Untangling confusion

Our friend Cal had nearly forty years of drug and alcohol addiction behind him when my husband, Bill, and I met him in a relationship course. He was only three weeks out of a two-year prison sentence for grand theft auto. As we got to know Cal, he told us that he and his uncle were the only two people in his whole family, for three generations, who were no longer drinking and using drugs. Cal was given alcohol when he was nine years old and became addicted very quickly. Alcohol and drug dependency were his life, until his experiences in prison helped him cleanup. He clearly wanted something different for himself.

Cal was taking PAIRS® (Practical Application for Intimate Relationship Skills) to learn healthy ways of being in relationship, to replace the confusion he had previously experienced with his family and others. He also attended at least three Alcoholic Anonymous meetings everyday. AA helped him examine his mistaken beliefs. Cal found the truth that "set him free" from his past mistakes which allowed him move towards a healthier, more honest, and loving relationship with himself. Cal was fully committed to a new way of living. As he integrated new experiences with healthy information about the world, he was more able to be who he really wanted to be. He's now married with a successful real estate business in the Midwest. He has never had a relapse into the harmful, self-destructive path he pursued for most of his life.

Even when behaviors are less destructive, we still need to be attentive to our thoughts, behaviors, and the effects of our behaviors, in order to shed light on our mistaken beliefs. Seeing that everything we do has an effect is living Awareness. Problems arise because our inner story and outer actions are out of alignment with what's real and right in front of us in the moment. We imagine all kinds of problems that don't exist, and then live as if they were real. We want things to be different than they are. Not questioning thoughts about the unknown future, making assumptions based on an unexplored past, we continue to run around like someone who thinks they have lost their glasses when they are on their nose all along. We are confused.

Let's say we have a dentist appointment and our children aren't getting ready to leave the house the way we believe they should. We feel frustrated in our attempts to speed them up. Frustration builds until we explode in anger. Without Awareness, we end up screaming, they end up crying, and everyone gets into the car upset.

With Awareness, we may feel frustration building, gently refocus the children, and keep things moving without exploding. Or, if we explode in anger, we can still use Awareness to notice our children's fear-filled faces. Then we can apologize right away. Everyone can feel a little better by the time we get into the car. Later, we can wonder about what belief caused the frustration, anger and explosion. Noticing our mistaken belief that our children should move the way we want, rather than the way they are moving, can free us up. Next time we can handle our frustration in a quieter, more loving manner. We might even plan more time to get into the car before appointments.

Noticing our actions, and their results, with less self-judgment, we can grow our ability to explore beliefs. With an Intention to stop exploding at our children, learning better communication skills with our spouse, or clearing up painful relationships with our parents, we begin to question the roots of our confusion. Then, with new clarity, we experience the relationship between our beliefs and what happens in our life.

This untangling of confusion can take time. Especially in the beginning, much Energy is needed to break through our habits of confusion. We begin to find fears we have never questioned and the process can be uncomfortable. Yet, as we continue to explore our habitual confusion we become more present, have more Energy, and our actions are more loving. And as we cultivate the Light of Awareness, the work gets easier.

5. The Light of Awareness

With one moment of Awareness, if we don't shut out the light, we begin to grow from our roots of confusion. We begin to use painful experience as fertilizer for our own nourishment. Just as flowers use fertilizer to nourish and support their growth, we can use our confusion and pain as fertilizer to nourish and support our growth. We are like the lotus flower that has long been a symbol of being awake. The lotus grows from the muck, and blossoms into a beautiful, fragrant, flower. We have the potential to grow from the muck of our cloudy, unconscious confusion, and blossom into a fully loving human being.

Being present, or aware, in any one moment, means we are being with *what is*. Whether we are enjoying the sight of a full moon reflecting on a lake, or sharing the moment of our child's first steps, we are with *what is*. That also means that when we are being self-critical, or impatient, we can be aware that we have pain-producing habits worthy of exploration.

Awareness is not always pretty, yet it is always new and fresh. Just as every breath is happening in the moment, every breath is fresh and new. Our Awareness helps us experience life as fresh and new in each moment.

It's good to remember that opening to the Light of Awareness is a process. Flowers have their perfect time to blossom, just as fruit ripens in its own time. We need to respect the step-by-step nature of our unfolding if we are going to grow in a healthy, loving manner.

Being with *what is*

To truly understand the possibility of meeting our experiences freshly, we must first notice how we do experience our life. We often see only what we want to see. We have filters made of our mistaken beliefs. We often don't notice what's right in front of us because of our inattention to *what is*.

It is as if we are standing at the sink doing dishes, and our son comes in with blood streaming down his face, from a cut because of a fight at school. We aren't going to see the truth (the blood) because we don't turn around and look at him. We keep doing the dishes. We say, "How was your day, Honey?" "Oh, it was okay, Mom. Nothing special happened…I'm going out to play soccer…be home in time for dinner!" "Okay, honey, see you later!"

Or, ever try to talk with someone about something "big," when they are reading the paper? They say, "Uh, huh," to everything we've said. Don't we live like this? So self-involved with our own lists, we don't see someone trying to read the paper? We make up stories about how they don't love us, because they don't stop reading when we're talking to them. Or, from the other side, we can be so self-involved with reading the newspaper that we don't see someone we love, standing in front of us, trying to communicate about something they care about.

Have you ever *not* heard someone respond to a question you have just asked him or her? Allowing thoughts to absorb us, focusing on what's ahead, or what just happened, we are barely present to what's right in front of us in this moment, as we rush from one thing to the next on our list.

So what can be done about these wandering, head-filling thoughts? Trying to stop or push them away is useless, exhausting, pain-producing work. Thoughts happen. And we are tremendously busy people, with loads to get done each day. We have to work, prepare meals, make plans, finish the proposal, get the children to the orthodontist, sign up them children for soccer and music lessons, check on the parents, and see friends!

Yet, *thoughts* about our work, relationships, vacation plans, or finances are not the problem. Thoughts come and go and we need to think things through sometimes. There is a physical, practical reality to our every day life and we need to attend to it. The problem is getting caught up, or velcroed, to some of our thoughts as they come up. Which thoughts are the most stressful? Which do you love to hold on to? Which thoughts become the foundations for the stories you tell yourself?

Imagining that we will be late for a sports event or meeting, we rush our children into the car as if someone is going to die if we are a few minutes late. Feeling like a failure, we throw out the eggs because the yolk broke, and waste perfectly good food. Yet, a "broken egg" offers a wonderful opportunity to relax and be open with *what is*! We can either respond with "whoops" and eat them anyway or say "!?!?#$%!" and throw them out. How do you feel when you make mistakes?

We all want to be happy, loved, and loving. Our rushed, impatient, unkind, unhappy behaviors come from unrecognized confused habits of thinking. This is simple to say and yet often not so easy to untangle. However, because we intrinsically want to find out what's true, be aware and happier, it is completely satisfying work when we do it.

Autobiography in Five Short Chapters

Awareness is truly an ongoing process. Here is a wonderful story called "Autobiography in Five Short Chapters" by Portia Nelson.[13] It makes the process of waking up clear— and funny in a wry, familiar way. We've all been here, and we continue to "walk down the street." Think of an issue in your life and see if you can recognize the chapter you are in.

Chapter I

I walk down the street.

> There is a deep hole in the sidewalk.
>
> I fall in.
>
> I feel lost. I feel helpless.
>
> It isn't my Responsibility.
>
> It takes forever to find a way out.

Chapter II

I walk down the same street.

> There is a deep hole in the sidewalk.
>
> I pretend I don't see it.
>
> I fall in, again.
>
> I can't believe I am in this same place.

---

[13] Nelson. Portia, "Autobiography in Five Short Chapters," retrieved from MH Sanctuary, December 11, 2005, Web Site: http://www.mhsanctuary.com/Healing/auto.htm

But it isn't my Responsibility.

It still takes a long time to get out.

Chapter III

I walk down the same street.

There is a deep hole in the sidewalk.

I <u>see</u> it is there.

I still fall in. It is a habit, but,

My eyes are open.

I know where I am.

It <u>is</u> my Responsibility.

I get out immediately.

Chapter IV

I walk down the same street.

There is a deep hole in the sidewalk.

I walk around it.

Chapter V

I walk down another street.

By Portia Nelson

The Light of Awareness saturates everything and provides the nourishment for all growth. It often takes time for us to open, though, and let the light into our lives. We can all be slow learners at times. You know how it is when you ask someone else to change? Maybe we ask them to call when they are going to be late, or put their clothes away instead of throwing them on the chair. Maybe we ask more than once or twice, and we end up in the same old argument. Isn't repeating uncomfortable interactions in a relationship, like falling into a hole again and again? At some point, we may begin to wonder about our responsibility. Noticing doing retakes, the Light of Awareness shines, and we can begin to recognize our role in creating the mess. Actually, we can think of repeated mistakes as *miss-takes*, like in the movies. It may be Take 5 or 5,0000 before we realize we are doing something to contribute to a difficult situation. It is often helpful to see a bit of Humor in the "movie" we've been writing, so we don't take our self too seriously!

With repeated discomfort, our Curiosity gets aroused. With Awareness, we can consider how to approach the "take" differently next time. Our understanding deepens. What can you do to make sure you avoid creating a messy situation again? Or to clear up an existing one?

A family mess

Each time we repeat a pattern and become more awake to our discomfort, we come closer to noticing what is happening in the midst of a situation. In the beginning, we usually notice a problem after it has occurred. Next, we realize we've been stuck in a mess and have somehow contributed to it. It doesn't really matter what kind of mess— it is just messy! Sometimes this may happen weeks, months, or years after living with the mess before we realize our Responsibility.

Our motivation and ability to pay attention grows as we notice the familiarity of discomfort, closer and closer to its creation. After a while, we notice right after it happens, and next we can be aware in the middle of the mess. Soon, we may be awake enough to notice the warning signs before we get stuck in that uncomfortable place. Eventually, we are aware enough to move in a new direction and live free of problems caused by that particular unconscious habitual reactivity.

When our two children were young, dinnertime was usually chaotic. I wanted to be the picture perfect Mom, gently inviting my children to cook dinner with me, smiling sweetly as they pleasantly helped cut vegetables and stir the soup. Hah! I was way too tired to be creative at the end of my day, and neither of them was interested in being with me when they had each other to fight with!

Emily and Jason would clamor for attention and scream at each other. Exhausted from tending to their needs, shopping, and managing the house all day, I had little Energy left to be patient, and put together a healthy meal. I hated it when my children whined, and I was afraid I couldn't handle it anymore. I felt irritated; I wanted them to stop. I wanted to be patient, but I was too tired to think of a way to help them with their feelings. Then I would blame myself for not being who I wanted to be, and react with irritation to their whiny voices. My nervous system was on overload, my patience went out the window, and my picture-perfect family scenario would look more like a sitcom everyone, but me, would find funny.

One day, I mentioned my frustration to Joanne, a friend and mother with decades of Awareness work herself. From our conversation, it became clear that I was telling myself "I can't handle this." Joanne suggested I notice what happened when these words went through the body/mind system. I found that having the thought and believing it, created an immediate downward spiral. The body/mind reacted as if I really couldn't handle what was going on!

Believing the message that I was falling apart, the body/mind reacted by saying, "Oh, is that what you want? Sure, we can fall apart for you!" I realized that falling apart was exactly what I had created.

Joanne suggested I give myself the helpful message "I can handle this," three times, the next time I felt like I was falling apart. I didn't have to wait long. The next day, Jason did something to put his big sister, Emily, over the edge. They both came whining to me for help. I felt exhausted and could feel pressure building inside me as if I would explode. My fists clenched shut with the Energy I was holding in.

Somehow I remembered what Joanne had suggested. This time, I repeated to myself, "I can handle this. I can handle this. I can handle this." It worked! I felt the body quiet down. I noticed the mind settle down as well. I had the necessary patience to help the Emily and Jason resolve their argument and finish dinner. Bedtime was sweet and loving that night for all of us, as we hugged and kissed goodnight. I was grateful to learn a fresh, loving way to respond to my children at the end of a long day. After countless takes, I had pulled myself out of *one* hole I never wanted to fall in again!

Over time, I came to realize that saying, "I am handling this," worked even better. I avoided falling into the "hole" by reminding myself, "I am handling this" as soon as stress began to build. It brought a smile when I said it. In contrast, my unconscious message "I can't handle this" was rooted in fear. I kept the cycle going until I was ready to ask for help. Joanne passed on useful information, and I could take another path. I knew what felt better, and I walked around the hole instead of falling into it again.

Expressing fears and physical irritation by having a temper tantrum, always makes the situation worse. Yet, it happens sometimes, doesn't it? Powerful feelings can get the better of us, and we lose patience, and say things or act in ways we wish we could take back.

Recognizing fears and painful feelings as they arise, we can feel the body's response to what is happening and be with our Awareness of *what is*. With fresh information about an alternative way of being, we can try new behaviors. We can experiment, for instance, with a healthy self-message like "I can handle this" or "I am handling this," even when we don't really believe it. With practice, we can learn to let fearful thoughts, physical irritation, and pain, pass through the body/mind, like clouds, without acting on the thoughts and sensations.

Every moment holds the opportunity for living with Awareness. Our loving, activated Intentions literally give us the Energy to keep going; to break through the crust of habits, so our flower of being can emerge into the full light of our life.

6. Desire for Change

It has been said that angels are waiting for us to open doors they set before us. They have all the time in the world and carry no judgment about how long it takes us to open the door. Can you be as patient and compassionate with yourself? At the sound of knocking at your door, can you imagine simply opening your door wide enough to see who, or what, is there? Can you imagine greeting change with a sense of adventure?

There is an immense gift that can come from staying open for even one moment. The Light of Awareness brightens *what is*. We see new possibilities, with fresh perspective. Staying present, instead of pushing away discomfort, or ignoring pain, we are stronger. We come to understand the reason we are stronger and clearer is because we have learned to use painful experiences to our benefit. We've stayed with *what is*; we've felt the discomfort and pain of our experiences, opened to change, and it has made us stronger. This is how one moment of Awareness, one moment of experiencing our door wide open, holds great possibilities for change.

Inevitability of change

Change happens. Every moment holds the birth or the death of every breath of every single living being on the planet! On a molecular level, constant change is happening, and there is nothing we can do about it. Of course, that is not the kind of change most of us are concerned with every day. Noticing new wrinkles in the mirror, a son or daughter getting a failing report card when you didn't notice any problems, or unexpectedly losing a job can all feel like unwanted change. Actually, even joyful change, like a child getting married, can create all kinds of challenges to our ability to deal well with change.

On a larger scale, chaos can strike a whole school district because several schools need to be closed due to a budget deficit; a hurricane or flood strikes and destroys our home and community, or terrorism suddenly becomes an actual threat in our day-to-day life.

Cultivating Awareness can help us handle the inevitable challenges we face. We practice being in the moment during ordinary daily life, and get better at being in the moment. Our past difficulties and habitual judgments can be set aside more easily. Even though it is challenging to deal with not knowing what will happen next, we have learned to trust the adventure. We don't get so entangled in fears that arise. When chaos hits, each moment can be fully experienced with presence. We can be more helpful to others and just get on with what needs to be done.

Practicing being in the moment, as we do when we meditate, we develop our ability to live with change. Our fear of change diminishes. Change can feel smoother and easier. We develop the courage to live moment-to-moment. Living in the moment helps us be open to whatever the next moment has to offer. Practicing being in the moment is one of the greatest gifts of meditation and Awareness work. It helps us experience the freedom that comes from living on friendly terms with the inevitability of change.

Opening to change

Years ago, I offered a workshop called Opening to Change, and people thought I was crazy. "Are you kidding?" they said. "Change is the last thing anyone wants!" Most of us resist change in day-to-day life. We often disregard a felt need to do some internal changes. We even discount warning signs, and deny the inevitable. We lock our doors to keep change out. We ignore the "visitor" as change knocks, then pounds on our door. Imagine what it would be like to greet the warning signs as welcome visitors. Then we can be more open to the gifts the visitor brings!

Recently I heard the story of a woman, Paula, who had lived in an abusive, pain-producing marriage for a long time. One month before I met Paula, her husband had been verbally cruel to their 14-year-old daughter as he had for many years. This time, Paula noticed the abuse and how her daughter's whole body seemed to collapse from the unkind words her father spoke. Paula stayed open to what happened, and rested in Awareness. She was able to see how destructive her husband was being to their daughter and made a healthy decision to leave the marriage. When I met her, she was happy with her decision and grateful for that one moment of Awareness when she truly saw a painful situation. Paula's openness allowed the space for creativity to change things for her daughter and herself. Awareness helped Paula clarify her confusion about her marriage, and she decided it was time to end it.

Think about this. Certain industries expect layoffs, and some people start job searches and explore options before they get a pink slip. Others do nothing until they are laid off, and then they realize it is time to get out there and explore new possibilities. Many others feel afraid, do nothing, get the bad news, get angry or depressed, and cut themselves off from the adventure life still offers.

This is not to say change is easy, or smooth, or should always be fun. The point is that life can be more like an action-packed adventure movie. When we are present, curious, and open to what's next, our attitude can bring us through difficult situations. That is what makes actors/actresses look like the heroes/heroines we adore. They seem to approach their artificially created, challenging situations directly, with complete presence of mind. We love to watch actors and actresses live heroically. Yet, we can learn to be authentically heroic and present in the face of change in our life. And it won't be from reading anyone else's script, either!

Being aware and open to what's next, we remain Balanced in the face of everything life hands us. When we are not aware, and something unexpected happens, we experience confusion, which often leads to pain and suffering, which in turn can lead us to our Longing to feel better. Noticing our response as we bump up against things we cannot change, we can learn to look inside for an answer to our situation. There is a synergy and simplicity to all this. How we respond to outside change demonstrates our ability to stay open, remain aware, and be with *what is*.

One such moment of Awareness and openness to change occurred for me a few years ago. My family was having financial difficulties. I had joined a few networking groups in the hope of propagating referrals for my guidance practice. One of my new networking friends, Sue, offered a Reiki healing session, and I accepted with delight. During the session, soft music and gentle healing Energy helped me deeply relax. Just before the session ended, I heard the words in my head, "You will make a forgiveness CD." I was astonished. I had briefly considered the idea, but had stopped short because of money issues. Now, however, the voice was clear. I knew I would move on the project. I realized I would just have to trust that the financial issues would be resolved.

I remembered that our daughter, Emily, had recorded a few songs at a private recording studio in town. I called the owner and he was glad to help us out. My husband and I worked on a script for the guided meditation on forgiveness, and we set a recording date. As the day approached, instead of being nervous, I grew excited. I loved the adventure of writing and recording a CD! Money fears could have stopped me, but with Awareness, there was nothing in the way. I felt clear about moving into the unknown with the CD project. And during the course of this project, our financial situation changed for the better. One moment of Awareness, coupled with openness to change, opened the way for an adventure worth living!

Naming practice

Mindfulness helps us be open and aware when change happens. Tools can be useful as we train our self to remain focused, or mindful, on whatever we are doing at the moment. One tool many have found useful is doing Naming Practice in the midst of our daily life. By simply naming what we are doing—"Washing dishes, washing dishes." "Walking, walking." "Driving, driving." —we are present. As we focus our attention completely on what we are doing by naming it, all thoughts quiet down. We are completely in the moment. And we may notice stress falling away as the body quiets down as well.

Healthy change can also come from naming unpleasant emotional states—"fear," "anger," "sadness," "loneliness," or "frustration." By bringing historically unconscious reactions into consciousness and simply naming them, we bring the Light of Awareness into the darkness. We can use this practice when we want to become more familiar with our emotional reactivity. It's also a useful practice when it's not the right time to explore the cause of our distress—like when we're in the middle of an argument, or as we are walking onstage to perform.

Naming our discomfort quietly to our self, we acknowledge *what is*, without pulling away, ignoring, or denying. Bringing Awareness to *what is*, we experience a healthy shift, or change. We go from being caught up in something painful to a sense of curiosity. With curiosity aroused, we may later explore the causes of our discomfort, finding freedom from our reactivity. But don't just take my word for it. Try it for yourself.

Personal check-in

Remember a time when you stopped yourself from saying something unkind to someone you love. What was the reason you stopped yourself? Perhaps you remembered a hurt look the last time you spoke that way. Perhaps you remembered feeling uncomfortable as you spoke. That memory helped you realize you didn't want to repeat that moment. You had a moment of Awareness and desired change. And the change happened when you consciously chose to stop yourself before hurting someone again.

Next time something changes, next time the expected becomes unexpected, notice how you greet the shift. Are you fearful or open? If you resist, notice the sensations in the body. Is there a curiosity about how you might be more open next time? Can this curiosity be called a desire for change? A desire for more Awareness? Ahhh!

7. Balance

What comes to mind when you think about Balance in your life? Ironically, ideas about living a balanced life have become one of the biggest stressors. If we managed to live up to the advice of countless magazine articles and life style experts, we'd be exhausted—always eating healthy, getting five half-hour sessions of aerobic exercise every week, 8-10 hours of sleep per night, and daily quality time (for oneself, loved ones, our community, and planet)—with weight training, meditation, yoga, fashionable clothes, meaningful hobbies, and excellent sex too!

Trying for perfect Balance, as defined by others, can keep us running around, filling up our life from someone else's perfect menu. We can get so caught up in living by prescription, we forget about simply being. We end up feeling stressed, dissatisfied, and wanting things we can't change to be different than *what is*.

Picture a seesaw on a playground. There is a tiny point of contact between the platform and the top of the solid base, isn't there? Think of that point of contact as the connecting point where our inner and outer worlds meet. That point of contact is where we act from our understanding. Our point of contact is where we live with Compassion, presence, and clarity—or judgment, impatience, and confusion.

The platform holds everything life brings our way. Life may cause the platform to tip up and down or sit quietly, and the point of contact remains constant. Being Balanced, we remain aware of our well-grounded base, no matter how smooth or out-of-control the platform feels as it interacts with us at our contact point.

Sometimes, of course, our contact point feels like we're living on a razor's edge between chaos and simplicity. At other times, our contact point feels like the stillness in the midst of a hurricane, while the changing winds blow the platform up and down and back and forth. Life can feel like a see saw, with a rhythm and craziness all its own. Balanced, we remain alert, a conscious point of contact between moments.

We've all experienced getting thrown off Balance in the rush of chaos. We forget we even have our base that is always grounded, aware, and Balanced. Yet, even as we feel lost in chaos, we really do have a strong, intrinsically balanced base of Awareness.

The working world

My husband, Bill, is a building contractor, which means he has a great opportunity to explore chaos and Balance every workday. Sometimes he has several people working on different jobs, with different needs, looking for his direction at the same time. Now, that is chaotic!

Bill typically works on two or three different jobs every day. His crew handles the carpentry aspects of jobs. Each job may also need an electrician, a plumber, a masonry crew, roofers, and a painter. Bill directs the whole job and makes sure that each subcontractor's job fits the next sub's piece, so the schedule comes together smoothly, the work stays on pace, and the renovation looks beautiful in the end. Most of the time, things do work out beautifully, but there are days that top the stressful chart, even for a person like Bill who has been meditating for many years. Bill says, "What makes the job most stressful, is when people don't do what they say they are going to do."

One day, Bill arranged to meet roofers at 8 AM on a job site. He made sure his crew arrived by eight, because they needed to work with the roofers at the same time. However, the roofers didn't show up, hadn't called, and couldn't be reached. Bill sent his crew off to pick up material at the shop, and get some work done on a job an hour away.

Then, he left to check out an emergency call from a mason at another job. The masons had been excavating a pathway for underground ductwork and had hit granite. They were anxious for Bill to arrive and figure out what to do next. Under Bill's direction, they tried to jackhammer the rock, but it didn't work. While they were discussing how to get the job done (maybe if they rented a special saw to cut away a piece of the rock), the roofers called. They wanted to know where he was. They had been delayed but were now ready to work. Bill had to reschedule the roofers since his crew had moved on because the roofers had been late. Now he was deep in problem-solving with the masons about how to break up the granite and save the ductwork. In the end, they did cut away rock with a rented saw, the ductwork fit properly, and the roof work eventually got done.

Later, Bill said, "That day I was good at staying with what is. If I can be honest and clear with customers and subs alike, the situation stays more Balanced, even when multiple confusions happen." So, when does Bill lose Balance? What happens when he forgets the aspect of his being that is always available, grounded, and clear? "The problems come up when I want things to be different than they are." Bill said, "That is when I lose my Balance. Then I may lose my temper with a subcontractor or a supplier, or hear myself complaining about my day at dinner. I know I can't plan for or control everything that is going to happen with all the subs and suppliers. If I adapt as I go, I stay in Balance."

Balance and chaos

With Awareness work and a meditation practice, we forget and remember to return to center, again and again—whether we are at our jobs, shopping, vacationing, or at home. After all, life is a lively personal collage. It includes self, others, passion, environmental conditions, housework, food, money, work, adventure, bills, physical activity, stillness, pain, violence, curiosity, humor, sorrow, creativity, sleep, fear, death, peace, laughter, joy, birth, denial, chaos, love, and more.

I think of Balance as a condition occurring when the different aspects of our life communicate well together. In other words, Balance is how we feel when we are loving, strong, and clear minded, no matter how chaotic internal or external factors can be. It is a condition that occurs with Awareness.

A curious aspect of Balance is that it actually exists within chaotic outer circumstance. We feel our way through as things become difficult in any kind of chaos. Our strengths and weaknesses are in full view. Chaos can remind us of what we can't control, who we don't want to be, and how we don't want to live. It teaches us whether we are living from our intrinsic Balance. That is the gift!

Chaos comes from nature in the form of floods, hurricanes, and earthquakes. Chaos is also the stuff we get caught up in when daily life is at its most stressful; preparing for a daughter's wedding or getting a family ready to go on a trip while you still have to go to work, and the children need help with homework and to be taken to after school sports, and shopping for a friend's birthday present, plus all the organizational work required to get away on vacation. Chaos.

Internal chaos is often created by our reaction to unexpected circumstances; like being fired from a job, being asked for a divorce, or getting sick. Loved ones dying, a beloved going to war, or living in the midst of war.

How we live with the chaos of our life defines our everyday experience. The picture of the flower portrays our wholeness. It shows how every interconnected part is essential for a balanced life. This is why Balance is the center point. It is a centering, internal experience. It is being still in the midst of the changing winds of our life, which informs our relationships with our family, our work, and ourselves. It is Awareness fully expressed. It is our true home.

Questions to ponder

Which aspects of the essential elements did you most strongly identify with? Which of the elements were more difficult to connect with? How would you rate your openness to change on a scale of 1-10 (10 being the most open)? Notice if that rating changes as you read on.

Chapter Two
The Flower's Six Petals

Blossoming into our wholeness

While admiring a blossoming flower, we often notice the beauty of each petal and how each one is perfect and interconnected with every other petal. The illustration of the Flowering of Inner Growth[14] reflects the beauty of each one of us fully blossomed. Each of the six petals is interrelated to all the others. And each petal is completely dependent on the others for Balance to be maintained.

Let's look at how the petals demonstrate our working with "miss-takes" in a loving way. For starters, a sense of Humor helps us remember human beings make <u>so</u> many miss-takes! We grow Compassion for the self when we refrain from self-blame and accusation, and we understand that our miss-takes are simply part of our learning process. Practicing forgiveness for our self, our hearts naturally expand to include others when they make miss-takes. By taking 100% Responsibility for our errors, Curiosity may be activated about how we might prevent similar miss-takes in the future. Creativity comes into play as we follow the inspiration that spontaneously arises from Awareness. Then, we can creatively move in a different direction, instead of repeating our miss-take the next time around. In the end, we feel Gratitude for the "miss-take," whether it was Take #2 or Take #588, because it has helped us grow from our experience.

---

[14] For the remainder of the book, the six petals, Curiosity, Humor, Gratitude, Compassion, 100% Responsibility, and Creativity will be capitalized, as well as the seven key elements from the illustration, to help the reader keep The Flowering of Inner Growth in mind.

Being who we want to be, who we long to be, the six petals of the flower demonstrate six aspects of our blossoming; Curiosity, Humor, Gratitude, Compassion, 100% Responsibility, and Creativity. With The Light of Awareness, our petals open, each petal playing an important role in our life, as we express who we really are.

1. Curiosity

I saw a bumper sticker the other day that read, "Curiosity explores magic. So ask questions!" I love the message because Curiosity and magic are intimately connected. Magic is what happens when we are actively curious! Have you ever watched a child explore the garden soil? Anything found is a treasure filled with delight. Every detail is explored. And the moment-to-moment detailed looking is enough! Curiosity fuels the whole exploration. There is nothing good or bad. Everything the child discovers is magical, just as it is.

Bringing an open Curiosity to our confusion, and our painful experiences, we allow a similar kind of magic into our lives. Curiosity gives us a chance to explore, free of needing to know how things will work out. Feeling the body's experiences, noticing thought, and not resisting or holding on to what's happening, we discover the transient cloud-like qualities of our feelings and thoughts. Something magical happens. Fears dissipate when we engage in openhearted Curiosity. Physical sensations may change and thoughts can pass through unrestricted. We simply notice what's happening in the moment.

Practicing Curiosity with Awareness, we don't feed our ideas of how things should work out. We carefully look at what's going on, because something of interest is attracting us. There is no need to make *what is*, different: to build up our feelings (as with self-pity or self-righteousness), or push feelings away (as with denial or self-judgment). We can experience our life as it really is without closing down, even when we are in pain or in unfamiliar territory.

Curiosity is not about having a right or wrong result. We haven't failed when things don't work out the way we want. Active childlike Curiosity is a kind of magical practice, because it brings openness with no expectations about how life, or the exploration of our troubles, should look. Curiosity requires openness. With Awareness, without setting up preconditions, we greet whatever comes up with a sense of adventure. That is magical!

Three and a half hours late

Kathy, a teenager, was exploring her boundaries. She had recently ignored family rules, such as coming home past curfew, not doing her homework on occasion, and leaving house jobs undone. Her mom, Georgia, had been getting more and more concerned about her daughter's well-being. She was worrying about the possibility of drug use, teen pregnancy, and failing in school.

The first time Kathy came home late from a date, Georgia greeted her at the door and accepted her excuse. She talked with her daughter in a mature, grounded manner and Kathy responded in kind. The next time Kathy broke a rule; Georgia noticed a little niggling feeling in her gut, yet she stayed calm and talked with her.

Lately, it was getting harder and harder. One night Kathy came in late one time too many, Georgia exploded, and then Kathy exploded. It ended badly.

Both mother and daughter were furious. Kathy didn't feel loved and trusted. Georgia felt angry and couldn't trust her daughter the way she wanted. Georgia had lost her temper and was angry with herself. Kathy got angry with herself for losing her temper as well.

Recently, Kathy went out on a date with a boy Georgia had barely met; just long enough to notice his spacey smile, and dutiful, polite demeanor with her, the parent.

While Kathy was out, Georgia brought Curiosity to the mess they had created. As the adult, she recognized her responsibility to find a new way to look at what was happening, in case Kathy came home late again. Georgia took the opportunity to openly explore how she might respond with Awareness next time. As it got later and later past curfew, Georgia tried to prepare for anything, yet part of her was still ready to explode.

When Kathy finally walked in the door three and a half hours late, Georgia felt her anger, managed to stay present, and her Curiosity was naturally aroused. She noticed her daughter's exhausted face and stooped tired body and wondered what had happened without jumping into judgment. Instead of opening with accusations, which had filled the mind for a moment, she paused and said nothing. Kathy collapsed in her mother's arms crying. She told Georgia how she had been walking for three hours to get home from her date's broken-down car. They had gone to a movie in a different town, and then started driving home. They stopped at a light and the car died, and wouldn't start again.

Kathy was scared to walk home alone, but her date wanted to stay with his car until the morning and she knew she had to get home. Cars passed, and she hid along the roadside, scared of something worse happening. Her cell phone wasn't working, and he'd forgotten his.

The openness that met Kathy when she arrived home, allowed a loving presence to embrace the situation. With Awareness, her daughter's upset condition was noticed, Curiosity aroused, and fearful, angry expectations dispersed. Awareness allowed Georgia to be with whatever came up.

What also happened is that Curiosity about previous painful interactions helped the next interaction be more loving. Curiosity was the key to this magical shift in Awareness. It changed a predictable closed-down encounter to something open and genuinely loving. Bringing an open, active Curiosity to our painful interactions, allows the possibility for transformation. Being present in the moment, painful interactions have room to change. Curiosity is magic dust we can sprinkle on stuck situations.

For now, Georgia was grateful her daughter was safe and sound, and grateful that she could be present when Kathy needed her to be. Perhaps, someday, the mother and daughter will laugh at what went through Georgia's mind that night before Kathy came home. Humor can be a powerful healer.

2. Humor

The ability to laugh at oneself, and the human condition, is important. Otherwise, we often take our self too seriously. We are, after all, all in this together. The Light of Awareness grows our ability to include an understanding of the bigger picture. When we can laugh at our self-judgments, as well as our judgments of others, our habitual negativity can be transformed. Humor lightens our perspectives and our hearts. Every time we smile and laugh, endorphins, our mood-enhancing hormones, are produced in the brain. They are part of the chemical reactions that give us the feeling of joy, love, and happiness. We need to smile. We need to laugh.

Humor reminds us we are truly connected with others. Good jokes show us how alike we are because we can see ourselves making the same mistakes as the person in the joke. Difficulties feel less personal. There are so many funny inconsistencies, challenges, and ironies in everyone's life. Laughing together, we are not alone in our struggles. Sometimes, we get caught up in the details of everyday life and forget to relax and enjoy each other. Yet, when we laugh at our own shortcomings, we lighten the moment and demonstrate not taking our self too seriously.

So, here, right in the middle of a very serious book, are some jokes and funny tales to pass along. A few have references, others are stories told by the famous Anonymous.

Who's hearing now?

A man goes to his doctor with a serious concern about his wife's hearing. "Doc, I tell you, it is terrible. I am really concerned about her hearing problems and she won't do anything to get herself tested. She won't listen to me, and thinks I'm nuts. What can I do?"

The doctor ponders for a moment and then tells him what to do when he gets home that night. The man leaves the office confident, having been given a solution.

Remembering Who We Long To Be

That evening, he comes home and he calls to his wife from just inside the doorway, "Honey, I'm home. What's for dinner?" He can see her through the dining room, at the kitchen counter with her back to him. There is no response from her. There is not even the slightest movement that would tell him that she's heard what he's said.

He's worried, but he remembers what the doctor told him. He walks into the dining room and calls again, "Hi sweetie, I'm home. What's for dinner?"

Still no response. No movement. Not a sound from her.

He's very concerned, but he knows what to do next. He walks across the dining room to the kitchen doorway. Once again, speaking loud and clear says, "Hi honey, I'm home. What's for dinner?"

Nothing. Not a single movement. Not a sound. Deep concern comes over him as he begins to realize the gravity of the situation.

Finally, he steps into the kitchen and stands behind his wife and yells into the back of her head, "Honey, I'm home. What's for dinner?"

His wife whips around and yells back, "Fried chicken, for the fourth !X!&#!! time!"

Shopping spree

A woman won a lawsuit against a U.S. department store for tripping over a child and breaking her leg. She claimed it was the store's responsibility to supervise children in their store. The child was her own two-year-old daughter!

From the Harper's Index:

Number of Nigerian motorists tested for insanity after they were caught driving against the flow of traffic in Lagos, Nigeria (2003)....608

Number of them found to be insane...1[15]

The drive for success

Amount a Canadian violinist was fined for practicing his violin while driving: $375. [16]

Four moms

Four moms are standing around talking about how important their sons are.

The first mom says, "My son is a priest and when he walks into a room, people say, "Good day, Monsignor!"

The second mom says, "My son is a Bishop and when he walks into a room, people say, "Hello, Your Grace!"

The third mom says, "MY son is a Cardinal and when he walks into a room, people say, "Good morning, Your Eminence!"

The fourth mom says, "Well, my son is 6'10" and 300 lbs of solid muscle. When he walks into a room, people say, "Oh! My God!"

---

[15] Funny Times, Inc., Cleveland, August 2004
[16] Funny Times, Inc., Cleveland, August 2004

Zen hot dog

Part I

A Zen Master walks up to a hot dog vendor and asks for a hot dog.

The vendor says, "What do you want on it?"

The Zen Master says, "Make me One with Everything."

Part II

The hot dog vendor hands him his order.

The Zen Master gives him a twenty-dollar bill.

The vendor takes it.

The Zen Master says, "Hey! Where's my change?"

The vendor says, "Change comes from the Inside."

It is good to take note of what makes us laugh sometimes. As we grow in Awareness, we may find that degrading, sarcastic, or cruel humor is no longer funny. There is still plenty of space for the kind of Humor presented here, without unnecessarily spreading misunderstanding, prejudice, and ignorance. It is also okay to be silly sometimes. Please remember to play, and to enjoy the many layers of absurdities, inconsistencies, and ironies in life.

3. Gratitude

Have you ever noticed how easy it is to feel grateful for the person who gets you to smile or laugh? It is easy to think of Gratitude as a feeling that comes from beauty as well: autumn in all its colors, a sunset, a flower garden in full bloom, a loving exchange, a delicious meal, and watching children play. It is not so easy, however, to find Gratitude in the hard, painful stuff of life, in the weeds of our personal gardens. How do we transform the pain in our self, in our relationships with others, and in the world? How do we transform feelings of frustration and anger, to Gratitude, Compassion, and healing?

During the fall, those of us who have flower or vegetable gardens lay them to rest for the winter. Our inner gardens, however, need the soil tilled year round. Gardens, and people, need sunlight, water, fertile soil, and loving attention to grow. If we see light as understanding, water as loving attention, and fertile soil as everyday experiences—both pleasant and difficult — we have a good base from which to observe our life garden. Then, we can begin to cultivate a garden that prospers.

If we see the painful stuff of life as "nutrient rich fertilizer," we must find a connected, healthy way of living with it. Our "fertilizer," or our everyday confused feelings and thoughts, are brought into the light through the exploration of these experiences. This light is called Awareness. It is with Awareness that the richest fertilizer becomes the richest Gratitude, a living expression of our personal garden.

Painful stuff

Let's look at some painful stuff. What happens when we don't get what we want? Do we wish the people in our life understood us better? Would we like our boss to have congratulated us for a job well done? Will the rest of the family ever stop dumping their dishes by the sink for us to wash?

When people in our life don't do what we want, or situations play out differently than we want, we often feel angry. Hurtful and blaming thoughts may be experienced; thoughts that can cause us pain as long as we believe them. At times, we all have impatient and/or unkind thoughts. It is what we do with these thoughts that show us exactly where we need to grow in our understanding.

In the midst of pain, can we be curious about our situation? Curiosity is what brings light to confusion.[17] Some valuable, non-judgmental questions we may ask to help trigger exploration are, "How am I feeding these upsetting (blaming, angry, etc.) thoughts? Do I want to continue to live like this? How can I untangle this confusion instead of continuing to feed it?

Turning the compost

While fighting, denying, or ignoring pain, we are confused. Confusion arises from the unexplored ingredients of our garden's compost pile, the stuff that has been sitting and cooking, never open to the full light of day. Confusion blocks the light of understanding that comes with Awareness. We get so caught up in confusion that we don't see it is time to turn the compost pile and reveal the inner workings.

This fermenting pile of pain-producing thoughts accumulates from a lifetime of unconscious decisions we've made about our world. All our interactions with others—as babies, children, younger and older men and women— have

---

[17] There is a continual interplay between being with *what is* and the work of going deeper. To think that being with *what is* is a passive state of continual acceptance is a misunderstanding. The active role of self-inquiry is essential to bringing clarity to our experiences. Being with confusion (when confusion is *what is)*, our heart's Longing for truth and clarity moves us towards active wondering about what we can do to feel better. Untangling confusion becomes the work, and the meditation of the moment.

contributed to our beliefs about our self and the world. If our parents are unhappy together, and we hear them argue about us, we might believe we caused their unhappy marriage. Or we might believe it is our job to make our parents happy if they get divorced. This is what naturally happens as we innocently react to what life has brought our way.

Can you imagine consciously turning your attention to your beliefs, to find out if they are true? By turning the compost pile, or exploring our pain-producing beliefs, we notice the fertilizer, weeds, and dead flowers. Working our inner garden can be sweaty, exhausting work, requiring Awareness, patience, honesty, and Compassion. The work is also bountiful. Our unfolding petals open us up to Gratitude. Gardening is like that.

Imagine yourself, standing before a beautifully blossoming garden. Imagine that you are the gardener, and the garden. The Gratitude for your being, the unfolding of all that is, is immense.

4. Compassion

Do you know what it is to be loving? Can you feel the difference between what is loving and what is not? Is there a Curiosity about the difference?

Compassion is the way unconditional love expresses itself. It is love in action, as love flows within the heart, and out into the world. With Compassion, when we sense another's pain, our hearts naturally open, and we embrace the other, with a loving, caring response. Sometimes more is called for. Sometimes simply being present and loving is all this is needed. It is our undivided, whole, clear, open, Awareness that embraces the other person, or situation, and knows what to do. Just being is enough. And when Compassion is present, nothing is in the way.

Opening the way

We can begin to wonder what gets in the way. Unless we question what gets in the way of an all-embracing, openhearted possibility of living, we will not discover our vast potential for living compassionately. It is our natural desire, our Longing, to be loved and loving. This desire is what gives us the Energy and motivation for more Awareness. Our Longing arouses our Curiosity to find out what gets in the way, what is creating the pain, and how to uncover more Compassion.

We can be so caught up in painful feelings, though, we are not aware of anything else. Thinking about whether we are being compassionate may be the farthest thing from our mind. At some point, we need to understand that a possibility for change exists. In order to change, there needs to be a deeply felt Curiosity about how to change our personal pattern of unloving behavior towards our self and others. With willingness to change our behavior, we are open to a new perspective. Then, we begin to open the way for change, as we notice what's happening, and allow judgment and blame to fall away. We also open the way by actively wondering, "What can I do to stop hurting myself and others?" We can notice how we explode or implode. We can notice how we take on more pain, and pass that pain to others, in a never-ending chain of unconscious reactivity.

Our stories

One way to begin uncovering Compassion is to understand how unexamined "stories" operate. You may be wondering what is meant by the word "stories." Think of your stories as the detailed expression of your personal history, how you think and talk about your situation or history to others. We all have particular ways of describing a relationship with a brother, sister, mother or father. You might think, "My father hated me," or "My sister was always mean." And, you probably find yourself describing your work in a particular way again and again. Listen to what you say about your parents, your partner, and your children. Can you see that the way you describe your life can be called storytelling? After all, what we say or think about our life, our story, often has a beginning, chapters, themes, characters, mishaps, drama, Humor, and adventures.

We are each the main character in a book called "The Story of My Life." We have written our stories throughout our lives. In living our life, we have looked for meaning, and connected experiences to beliefs, which fit our understanding at the time. All the people, places and things in our life are tied together in our story— just as a writer of fiction creates a story line, main characters and themes. And, we are usually attached to our interpretation of our story.

Some parts of our stories are plainly neutral accounts of history and other parts are based on our innocent, unexamined, often pain-producing interpretation of what happened. When a parent is abusive, a child may mistakenly believe it is his or her fault. This interpretation, made in a child's mind, is not usually questioned.

The child can grow up carrying the belief that he was responsible for, or deserving of the abuse he experienced.

Or, perhaps, parents get divorced, and children feel it is their fault for not being good enough. Or a parent dies, and there was an argument, and mean things were said before the parent died. The child might feel responsible for his parent's death.

The heart's natural ability to feel and express Compassion is blocked by unloving, untrue beliefs about the self, others, and the world. Our stories keep the heart shielded until we begin to explore our mistaken beliefs—beginning to uncover what's true, gently, carefully, one experience-at-a-time, and one mistaken belief-at-a-time.[18] Finding out what's true, the protection around the heart naturally softens. We begin to feel our intrinsic capacity for Compassion, expressed by living with a less defended heart.

Ray Charles

Do you know the story of Ray Charles, the singer? According to the movie, *Ray*, he experienced a terrible trauma as a young boy. He witnessed his younger brother drowning and he couldn't do anything to save him. We might assume from the movie, that Ray felt terrible guilt about his brother's death. Shortly afterwards, he went blind. Ray suffered from nightmarish delusions when he grew up, and became a heroin addict to cover up his pain. Ray was able to recover and create a healthy life only after he hit rock bottom from the heroin addiction. Checking himself into a hospital, Ray found the necessary physical,

---

[18] For some of us, the attachment to our whole story can fall away in a moment of Awareness.

psychological, and spiritual support he needed to face his pain and hopefully, stop blaming himself for his brother's death. His interpretation of his life story changed to include Compassion for himself, and he was able to live a life free of the addiction, which had tormented him for so long.

Mistaken beliefs continue to create confusion for all of us, if they are left unexplored. As with Ray Charles in the movie, our unconscious interpretations of our personal history continue to live in us and affect our daily life—even though they are based on the past, may be incorrect, and may have no relevance to what is happening right now. These unconscious stories can wreak havoc on our emotional, social, physical, mental, and spiritual condition until they are brought to light.

Expanding our view

As we begin to explore our stories, we notice beliefs we have blindly accepted. By gently examining our stories and beliefs with no blame, no accusation, no judgments, we find our heart opening a bit. Feeling more open, we can carefully wonder what is true. We can stay with whatever comes up. Then we see a slightly bigger picture. We can appreciate an expanded, less shielded, and more compassionate view of our own life story.

As we notice our prejudices and consciously explore our beliefs, our heart also includes people we have kept out. People with different political views, of a different culture, religion, race, sexual orientation, or financial situation are embraced, instead of excluded from our heart. Continuing with honest exploration of our beliefs, we see more about why we're in so much pain. We see more of why others are in pain. Our capacity to feel Compassion, our intimate interconnection and interdependence with others, grows.

Confusion based on our unexamined beliefs and stories creates and sustains world problems, such as war. If we look at what is happening in the world, we can assume that terrorists who carry out their mission are deeply confused about what is loving. We hear they think it's the right thing to do, and that they believe their actions will have a positive effect on the world. The stories the terrorists tell themselves, and that others tell them, must suppress any Compassion for the people they kill.

We can see the potentially terrible effects of not examining our own personal stories, not because we are in danger of becoming terrorists, but because we also create pain from unexplored, unconscious beliefs.

Compassion is uncovered when we embrace a way of living with the practice of Awareness at its core. Focusing with Awareness in the present moment, we are joining heart, mind, and body. Being present, we are awake and alive to whatever is needed. The heart will always be there, ready for compassionate response, whenever it is needed. It is the way things work. It is the way we are made.

5. 100% Responsibility

Many of us heard the word "Responsibility" in a negative way as we were growing up. It was usually connected to a whole list of things we felt forced to do. We may have developed a negative reaction to the word because the list was so long— homework, chores, work, being nice, saying "thank you," "I'm sorry," etc. Here's an opportunity to discover a new attitude about the word

Responsibility: Taking the word and breaking it into two main parts, we get response-ability. Imagine having the ability to respond appropriately to what is in front of us. That is all there is to it. Simple, but not always easy!

In order to respond appropriately, we need to be clear and present with what is in front of us, without mental and emotional baggage weighing us down. Experiencing this kind of alert, spontaneous clarity happens as we cultivate Awareness. Eventually, we see something needs doing and we respond. If we're on a walk and see litter, we pick it up. If a man stumbles in front of us at the grocery store, we reach out to help him. If the children need some fun time with mom, the dishes are left until later. We respond in the moment to what's needed.

Friends visiting when Emily and Jason were young often commented (once they knew me well enough) how grateful they were my house looked lived-in. Sometimes I wondered if it was their way of saying the house was a mess. Toys were on the floor, and dirty dishes were often sitting by the sink, but I was comfortable enough with the disorder to have friends visit anyway. Our home was happy and I hoped my "mess" gave them permission to relax a bit about housework, and enjoy their children more.

Being responsible is another aspect of being aware. The ability to *just respond* happens when we're aware. We move with clarity and kindness instead of *just reacting*, by lashing out or speaking unkindly. When we're aware nothing is in the way of our response. We can thoroughly explore a situation. Curious about what's true, we learn not to blame our self or others, or to decide that someone is right or wrong. Feeling open to whatever comes up, can we ask our self,

"What's really going on here?" Being open and aware, we know what it means to *just respond*.

Forgiving the boss

Claire came to my series of three classes on Awareness work. She felt stuck about a painful issue at the office. Her boss was being unkind and verbally abusive. Claire had fibromyalgia and knew the stress from work was contributing to her poor health. She wanted to feel better, yet working with her boss was very difficult. She was afraid to speak to her boss. She was blaming her boss for her misery. Claire was not being "responsible" for her own health and well-being at work.

We worked with forgiveness the first class. Claire shared her story about her boss before our meditation. Afterwards, she reported that she felt better about her boss. Two weeks later, at the beginning of the second class, Claire shared that she had forgiven her boss, and herself, but it was still difficult to go to work in an abusive situation. We practiced a Compassion meditation, and she said at the end of the session, "That was hard work, but good to do."

Two weeks later, at the outset of the last class, Claire arrived for class with a big smile on her face. "I quit my job!" she said. She didn't know what was next; yet taking Response-ability for her well-being helped her do what was best for her health. Her fibromyalgia was better, and she was glowing with the joy she was feeling. Bringing Awareness to her story, and forgiving her boss, Claire expanded her ability to feel Compassion. She responded to what felt 100% good for her with clarity and honesty, and quit her job. Confusion was no longer in the way. Claire discovered the best course of action. She took Responsibility for her own health and well-being.

Being responsible includes being aware whenever someone treats us poorly, and noticing our reactions. That is what Claire experienced when she was ready. She was able to respond with clarity once blaming her boss was completely out of the picture.

Being 100% responsible for our behavior, not only means being clear about what to do, but also what not to do. One example of not being responsible is blaming. When we blame, we are responding with a closed heart to a person or situation. We are also tightly velcroed to our limiting beliefs about right and wrong. Then, how can we respond to our children with kindness when we are interrupted? Or how can we have patience with a parent who repeats a story we have already heard a dozen times? Unless we loosen the hooks that keep us velcroed to our thoughts, and expand our understanding to the bigger picture, we stay stuck in confusion—and unable to act with Response-ability.

It is good to see clearly when someone else is experiencing a confused, pain-filled moment. Instead of closing our heart, we can respond by checking into how we are feeling, and explore our response-ability in the situation. With Awareness, we are 100% Responsible, and nothing less than 100%. We may even find Compassion taking the place of blame again and again.

6. Creativity

I tuned in to a national radio program once and heard an author speak about his book on Creativity. I was surprised to hear him say that the silence out of which Creativity arises, is different than the silence we experience in meditation. That is not my experience. Any interpretation of silence limits our understanding of it. The wondrous openness of silence is where all Creativity is born. Silence just *is*. Silence is the fertile ground of all that is and each person expresses Creativity differently. That is part of the wonder of Creativity.

Inspiration[19] for everything creative arises out of silence. Just as Compassion is unconditional love in action, so is Creativity inspiration's expression in the world. With Awareness, our usually busy mind is quiet enough for us to notice when inspiration happens. Then we experience inspiration directly and either move with the invitation or not.

Experiences with inspiration can differ from one person to another. Awareness of breathing, fully listening, seeing, touching, tasting, sitting, or actually being fully present in the moment with *anything*, offers us the opportunity to live from inspiration, instead of our confusion. That's how Awareness helps us find a loving, creative way to be with life's joys and challenges. It opens a space for inspiration to be recognized, or spontaneously acted from.

Most of us think of Creativity in a limited way. We imagine that the only creative people are those of us who are artists, composers, chefs, writers of fiction, and poets. Creativity includes everyday acts of putting together a dinner, sitting attentively in meditation, taking a break from work by going for a walk, and realizing we can stop arguing in the middle of an argument. One author puts a

---

[19] Inspiration, as it is meant here, implies a direct experience of what is loving and what is not, for oneself. It should never be mistaken for the voices deeply confused people hear that direct them to harm themselves or others.

paper bag over his head to eliminate distraction and generate new stories for his next book.

We are actually completely creative beings every moment, whether we are aware of it or not. Our problems arise when we are not aware because then we create from our pain-producing conditioning rather than the beautiful, loving, openness that inspiration and creativity bring into our life.

The more we live with Awareness, the more we understand the immense part that Creativity plays in our life. We simply practice being with *what is*. As time goes on, with less attachment to our conditioning, we realize that every moment lived with Awareness is a moment filled with Creativity. Then, we experience the joy of Creativity permeating every aspect of our life. And we are no longer engaged in the endlessly exhausting, and impossible work of making the world fit our limited view.

During meditation time, a new idea about how to help a difficult situation at work may arise. Or, unexpectedly, the title of a book could pop up during a walk in the park, and we find our self on an exciting book-writing adventure never seriously considered before. Maybe we notice our confusion during an argument, and we begin to wonder about what's happening. In a moment of Awareness, out of the deep silence, we understand something differently, and are inspired to make changes in our situation. Miraculously, we know what needs to be done. Creation!

Hearing in the fog

Practicing being focused in the moment helps us quiet down inside, and allows our lives to unfold so that inspiration and Creativity can play a bigger part.

To illustrate, a few years ago, there was a terrible accident on a densely fog-darkened highway. Many cars smashed into one another as people approached the original accident, not sensing the impending danger.

One woman shared her story on the radio. She was driving along, carefully, intensely paying attention to the road because of the fog. She reported hearing a voice tell her to pull over and stop. Responding spontaneously, even though she had never heard a voice like that before, she pulled over. When she got out of the car, she could clearly make out shapes ahead of her on the highway. As she walked closer, she realized there was a terrible pileup and so she started waving oncoming drivers to stop. With inspiration, a woman saved many lives and cars that night because of her loving, decisive, and creative action in an emergency.

An experiment

One often hears poets and writers speaking of their muse, their inspiration, which arises from the silence. Experiment with entering the silence. Drop all stories of what happens there, especially the hope for inspiration, and simply rest with *what is*. Notice thoughts coming and going. Actively wonder what exists before a creative thought. Wonder what exists before all thought. Stay with this for a few minutes. Be gentle with yourself when you are done. And stay open, because this experiment could become part of your daily life.

A reminder

Becoming clear about who we long to be helps us as the challenges of relationship, money, health, housing, or work, greet us. Once we begin to be aware of our "roots of confusion," and explore what keeps us confused, all the petals of our flower gradually open and express in our life. As we notice good changes, we are energized to continue. We need to activate all of our "petals"—Curiosity, Humor, Gratitude, Compassion, 100% Responsibility, and Creativity—when we want to change and break through our pain-producing habits.

Stepping into our adventure means we have to be willing to experience and explore discomfort. We have lived with some discomfort for so long it feels like "normal." Take a moment to think of one difficult relationship in your life, that you have been accepting as the norm. Are you comfortable with it? How can you find a more loving way to be with yourself and the other person?

Remember that you already contain all the elements you need to be a beautiful flower, whether you are a rose, a tulip, carnation, peony, cactus, dandelion, or violet. A flower needs light, moisture, and the right fertilizers to blossom. You need to be curious about Awareness (the light), have the Desire for Change (the moisture), and have the Intention to see through fears and mistaken beliefs (the fertilizer) to help the seed of you grow in Awareness of all that you are.

Part II

What Gets in the Way

"Awareness is not always pretty."

Chapter Three
Exploring Beliefs

Growing into a Healthy Flower

Any kind of gardening takes work. All unexplored mistaken beliefs sabotage our blossoming. Uprooting the sabotaging weeds of confusion requires doing our work with Awareness. The potential of our seed experiences, coupled with the fertilizer imparted by the confusion surrounding us, provide the perfect material for our blossoming. By actively engaging with our inner life, we tend the flowering of our full human and spiritual potential—an emotionally healthy, loving, balanced, present, joyful, human being.

1. Belief Work

Beliefs are our interpretations of thoughts and experiences that we hold onto without questioning. Beliefs happen as a conditioned expression of our human existence. From the time we are born, we have the capacity to receive all the love the world has to give us. Some of us come in screaming, some smiling, and all of us are basically open, needing, and deserving to be loved. It is our birthright. Parents love us, yet they often act in confused ways that confuse us. We interpret our parents' behavior and the causes of their behavior, based on the limited understanding of our child-mind. Our interpretations develop into a whole belief system because these interpretations remain unquestioned and often misunderstood.

What Gets in the Way

As we grow up our belief system expands to include the self, our family, and the rest of our world. Being attached unquestioningly to any belief, whether a belief is so-called positive or negative, creates potential pain and confusion. Our attachment to a misguided belief prevents us from living directly from the heart because our confusion is in the way.

For example, being attached to a belief like "I am wonderful" creates pain and confusion, if we get caught up in our own importance and treat other people poorly. Other beliefs, such as "I have no worth," "I am stupid," and "I am a failure" keep the heart shielded. Living from these deeply painful beliefs, we unconsciously create chaos and confusion. We seldom question these mistaken beliefs. We can also draw misguided, unconscious, conclusions from on our beliefs; such as life is all about me because I am so wonderful, or life is confusing and painful and there's no way out.

It seems that we need to experience pain from our mistaken beliefs in order to wake up. In fact, our lives can feel like a bumper car ride at the amusement park. Endlessly bumping up against what doesn't work, we continue living confused, distracted lives until we realize we can do something about it. Then, we can wonder about what's next, and how to help things change for the better. Once we are looking for a healthier way of being, a more loving way of being, a moment of Awareness may give us a fresh perspective. And we may find our self on a new path.

Every one of us started out blameless and spotless. All judgments fall away when seen in this light. It can be a tremendous relief to realize this for one self. Once we understand that all beliefs stem from our *innocence*, how can we continue to hold judgment against our self and other people? Accepting our intrinsic purity, we can explore our pain-producing confusion with more openness. And then, we can continue the exploration throughout our life.

Healing with Awareness

My mother was mentally ill. Whenever she held me, I felt her need to be held, rather than her loving me. I grew up feeling lonely and believed I was being left out. Now, I understand that I was leaving myself out. When a friend doesn't call me, it doesn't mean a friend doesn't like me. It can mean they are busy or out of town. If I want to see someone I call him or her. Simple. Now.

I was twenty-seven when I moved to Ithaca with my boyfriend, Bill, now my partner and husband of thirty years. I was ready for change. I had lived with a young man for six years and we had gotten caught up in our fears and strong, scary emotional outbursts. I wanted someone quieter who wouldn't yell at me, throw a cast iron pot on the floor, or put his fist through a wall. Bill felt clean emotionally, after the chaos I had come from. He was emotionally under control and I felt safe.

However, when Bill and I were past the honeymoon time, I began to feel lonely and cut off again. My own negative self-talk, blame and judgment kept getting in the way of being happy. The friction in our relationship pushed me to see a psychotherapist. I was in pain and I realized I needed help.

My mother had been in psychotherapy my whole life, so I knew it was available. I went to a good psychotherapist until I understood my family history better. I also cried and screamed and felt sorry for myself, until I had my fill of self-pity. I eventually uncovered enough of my pain-producing beliefs to learn

What Gets in the Way

that it was my Responsibility to deal with my feelings and not dump them on others. I alone was responsible for my feelings, whether they were feelings of well-being, sadness, or anger.

Thankfully, my husband Bill was interested in Zen Buddhism and opened the door to a whole new possibility for me. I learned I was capable of living an aware, compassionate, and grateful life. Since I was not living that way, I realized I had some work ahead of me.

Many mistaken beliefs haunted me. I still got angry easily. I still felt cut off and lonely sometimes, even though I understood my family history. Over time, my feelings of self-pity and being left out arose less often, with less intensity, as negative beliefs fell away. I exploded with words of anger less often. I ached to experience a loving life, freely sharing the love I knew was possible.

Actually, it took years of Awareness and meditation to break the habits of self-pity and feeling left out. There were times when all I had was the moment-to-moment work of Awareness. Sometimes I felt terrified as if I was living on the edge of a precipice, and knew I had to jump into the unknown. Or, I would suddenly be aware of feeling tightness in my chest, understand it was emotionally based, and be curious about what had caused it. Or, in the midst of an argument with Bill, I would feel attached to my belief about my being right and his being wrong. With a moment of Awareness, I was able to experience a distance from my attachment, and things would go more smoothly. I needed correct information to clear up the confusion left by my family upbringing, my educational experiences, and the culture I grew up in. New information about the possibility of a compassionate, wise, and joyful life helped me have faith in something more loving than what I had known as a child. I was inspired to keep going.

The exploration of my painful habitual responses to unconscious beliefs hasn't come to a stop. Sometimes impatient feelings sneak up on me, especially when I'm tired. I am very familiar with the sensations of anger rising. I've had countless opportunity to say "No thank you," to blaming and Poor Me thoughts. I find myself apologizing more readily.

There is no *one* time better than another. When our time is ripe, we feel the need for change. Wanting a new perspective may arise as we notice the pain on a friend's face when we've been sarcastic. Listening to the news may trigger a deeply personal questioning such as, "How am I contributing to the mess the world is in?" Experiencing pain, touching into our heart's Longing, and having useful information about how to be with our discomfort, we can move towards being more loving and compassionate.

Sometimes it takes a life-changing, extreme event, to shake us into a new perspective. Many of us have heard of a heart attack victim who is willing to make dramatic lifestyle changes he would not have considered before the attack.

The heart attack

Larry, a visitor to my meditation class, is one of those people you hear about. He was 42, overworked, ignoring a viral infection, eating poorly, and drinking too much. Finding himself in the hospital emergency room with congestive heart failure, he told the class he saw the defibrillator coming at his chest and asked, "You're going to put me to sleep first, right?" "No," the doctor said, standing over him with the defibrillator in his hand. "We can't take the risk with all the crap in your system, so hold on!" The doctor proceeded to electric shock Larry's heart three times while Larry felt helpless and much too awake. Larry told the group, "No one should ever have to experience *that*. That is why I tell my story, to help others understand how important it is to find a healthy way to live *before* they reach the emergency room!"

Fortunately, Larry had a cardiologist who understood how to help Larry make the necessary lifestyle changes and begin a life with more Awareness. Larry's heart attack pushed him to uncover at least some of his mistaken beliefs—that it was okay to drink a lot, work so hard, and party so much. Now that he is more aware and meditating, he can continue to uncover additional mistaken beliefs that get in the way.

However, even without a "big one," we can purposely take note of everyday confusion as a pointer to wake up. In the beginning, that often means uncovering one pain-producing belief at a time. Focusing inwardly, without judgment, we can notice the confusion and pain right here! One time one mistaken belief may be uncovered. At another time, a whole network of beliefs can fall away in a moment of Awareness. Starting with our self, we begin to heal our own life. We don't have to continue contributing to the mess so much of the world is in.

Noticing and being curious too

For example, we might notice how we feel in our troubled relationship with someone at work. We can be curious about the thoughts affecting our relationship, and wonder how we can be more open and compassionate. At

What Gets in the Way

home, when our partner asks us to get up early and take the car to the mechanic, how do we respond being asked to do something we'd rather not? Can we be curious about whether we are smiling upon getting up, grateful to help, or is there something in the way?

What happens as we go from simply seeing a pile of laundry to "I shouldn't have to do this," or "Darn, she should've gotten this done. Now, I have to do it!" Can you wonder what gets in the way of doing what needs to be done?

We already have beliefs and we are going to have thoughts. It is not thought that causes a problem. It is our *habitual reactions* to unexamined thought that keeps us entangled in continual knots of confusion. Unconsciously reacting from an unexamined thought—I can do this later. I hate dusting. I hate doing the bills—keeps a cycle of confusion alive; as we unconsciously go from confusion and unexamined thought, to habitual reaction, pain and confusion, to habitual reaction, and on and on.

Finding a new relationship with thought

Simply put, it is our relationship with our thoughts and beliefs that determines how we live our life, and how we feel. We can't stop thought in our daily life. However, we can develop a much healthier relationship to our thoughts.

We can be aware of thoughts about resistance and judgments (especially regarding chores, relationships, and professional opportunities), and let them pass through us, like clouds passing through a clear blue sky. By not believing them or getting hooked by them, we are free to see what's right in front of us with clarity. If the clothes need washing, and we have time, we do them. If we don't have time, later will be okay. If something needs doing right away, we just do it, instead of putting it off or thinking it is someone else's responsibility. We can understand when it is only a *thought* about resistance, self-centeredness, or blaming someone else.

Mistaken beliefs seem to be hardwired into the body/mind system, and unconsciously create all kinds of reactivity that requires exploration. Thoughts have no power unless we unquestioningly believe they are true. Being convinced that a thought is true creates a belief. However, catching a pain-producing thought as it happens, we can let it go. There is a delicious, open space experienced as we let thoughts pass through the mind. And then we can move with more openness, clarity, and presence.

Family values

At one point in my life, I realized that my belief, "I am responsible for all the housework," was not true. It was time for my family to reflect the change appropriately.

I called a family meeting. Bill and Jason agreed to a weekly job chart to clean the floors and dishes, and our laundry got done "whenever" (whenever we needed our clothes!). We cleaned up better when people were coming to visit, and shared a more general cleaning every two weeks or so. The rest of the time, we were doing the best we could; Jason with sports, schoolwork and a job, Bill with work and soccer coaching, and me, with my work. The chart reminded me when I was responsible for sweeping. And, although the dishes didn't always get done before bedtime, when I remembered Bill's or Jason's busy day, I let my knee-jerk criticism pass through the body/mind without getting caught up in it.

Family chores, which were traditionally a part of my job description, now required negotiation and planning in order to get the job done. And it worked!

Prior to learning how to focus with Awareness, anger and frustration may occupy a good deal of our time. At times, we may believe we are a failure, can't have friends, or can't keep a job. We may unconsciously blame others for our situation. We may become numb to our feelings as a protection because we unconsciously believe there is too much pain for us to handle.

Bringing a gentle, active Curiosity to our inner life opens the way for more Awareness. Things begin to change. Previously unexamined feelings may begin to surface. Frustration, anger, fear— actually any of our painful experiences— can be noticed and gently wondered about.

Many people say, "I can't hear my thoughts, how am I supposed to know what I believe?" If this is an issue for you, let the question sit there and explore what comes up with openness. Allow Curiosity to grow, without needing an immediate answer. Being curious in this way allows Awareness to quietly deepen.

2. Going Deeper

Many of us skim over the surface of life, afraid of falling in and going deeper. If we are going to find long-lasting happiness, we need to be aware when something isn't working. We need to be curious about what we can do differently. Then Curiosity takes us deeper. Bringing Curiosity to the beliefs creating so much of our pain, we explore our stories, and uncover our blind spots—even if in the beginning we have no idea what those beliefs may be.

With Awareness we are right in our life: we are no longer surfing along the top. Being aware embraces all our feelings, and our reactions, without pushing either away. We are with *what is* without necessarily going into reaction. Noticing discomfort—whether we call it anxiety, fear, frustration, or anger—we can feel what's happening and softly, quietly, wonder what's going on, without pushing or trying to change anything. A shift happens in the midst of wondering.

Through the deepening connection with our inner life, and our interaction with nature, other people, and the so-called civilized world in which we live, we learn that the body's messages point us to what's true and real. Physical sensations are "pointers." They are created from a multiplicity of interactions with thought, belief, and sensory contacts with the world.

When approached with Curiosity, we can explore sensation with openness. Sensations can be pleasant, unpleasant, extremes of both, and neutral. Sensations may be described as warm, cool, tightening, relaxing, tickling, moving, stillness, full, empty, antsy, electric, ad infinitum. As long as there is Creativity, there will be new ways to describe how we feel.

Once we recognize physical sensations as pointers, we realize we have a built-in message system worth studying. One time, a little tightening in our belly may be telling us we believe something untrue. We might even feel the same sensation when someone else is telling us something untrue. Another time, our throat tightening may mean we are holding back angry words. A feeling of openness in the chest in a historically difficult situation may let us know we are on the right path.

Listening and responding to the body's message system with Awareness helps us sort out what is loving and what is not because the body knows the difference. However, the body may know the difference and the mind may step in and incorrectly interpret what's happening. Going deeper, we develop a trust in the process of exploration and keep going. Untangling confusion about what is true is part of the work. That's what this work is really all about. Finding out what's true for oneself!

Exploring blind spots

What is a blind spot anyway? Simply put, it is whatever is in the way of clarity. Clarity allows us to have a healthy distance from our experiences and feelings so that we can know what feels true and what feels untrue, even in the midst of chaos. Mistaken beliefs are like the layer of dust that covers our windows at home, creating blind spots. Have you looked through glass after it has been thoroughly cleaned? You notice all the dust, spots, and gunk, are gone. Everything you see seems fresh and clean, spotless. We can experience that kind of inner clarity when we shed light on a blind spot, and explore a mistaken belief to find out what is true.

I had an easy blind spot one day when I went shopping for charcoal at our local food co-op. The charcoal had been piled by the front door the last few times I was there, but when I looked this time, I didn't see any. I asked a store worker if we were out and she said there were two bags there earlier. I followed her to the front of the store, where I believed I had looked, and two bags were right there. Just where I had a blind spot! I got teased a bit for that one.

Blind spots created by belief are really no different than that bag of charcoal. We don't see them until we do. Knowing we *all* have them though, helps us look for signposts pointing the way. Going off unhappily to work each morning could be fertile ground for blind spot exploration. Or, engaging for years in the same argument with a parent could point to blind spots for both people involved, although we can only work on our own confusion. We might be cut off on the highway and have an anxiety attack after the event is over. Whatever's behind the anxiety attack could also be called a blind spot.

Have you ever been repeatedly attracted to people who are selfish, irresponsible, or neglectful? Perhaps they behave in self-destructive and violent ways with themselves and others. A blind spot may create an unexplained attraction, again and again, to the same kind of unhealthy friend or lover. Because this kind of blind spot can be thickly layered and difficult to "clean up" on our own, it is good to get help exploring the beliefs that keep us attracted to people who behave in obviously unhealthy ways. Clearing up blind spots that attract us to unhealthy relationships, and/or keep us in them, help us make better choices in relationship later on.

It often takes time to know what's in the way of clarity. Our immediate judgments can be colored by a whole lifetime of unconscious memories and experiences. Blind Spots, or mistaken beliefs, darken our perceptions, so that we don't see the world as it actually is. And we live much of our life unaware that we even have them!

What Gets in the Way

Hey you! Over here!

The body has its own way of helping us learn about our blind spots. Uncomfortable feelings, or sensations in the body, are useful pointers to the thoughts and beliefs we haven't seen. It is as if the body is saying, "Hey you! Over here! Over here." Follow these directions attentively and perhaps you will get a glimpse into your blind spot.

Noticing discomfort doesn't mean we need to do anything with our sensations. Not needing to *do* anything is what Awareness allows. For the moment, we are aware of what is happening and that is enough. Our Awareness guides us in the moment-to-moment exploration of *what is*, as strong sensations pass through without taking hold. We can feel the sensations without needing to act on them. With 100% Awareness, there is no judgment or blame, no right or wrongness of what we are feeling. It just is. We are handling it. We are present with *what is*. We begin to notice the changing nature of sensation. They run through the system without resistance when we refrain from "feeding" the story.

With practice, we learn to trust Awareness. Our open exploration of *what is* allows the possibility for inspiration to arise about the cause of our discomfort. And we can move in a healthy direction, untangling confusion along the way.

Late for dinner

The process of unraveling mistaken beliefs can take a long time. We need to cultivate patience with the process. For example, my husband, Bill, used to have a blind spot in his understanding of something I believed was important. When we first lived together, I asked him to remember to call if he was going to be late for

What Gets in the Way

dinner. He would stay late at work and not call home to let me know that he'd be late. His blind spot was in the way of understanding my feelings, and calling. He would come home late without calling, dinner would be cold and I would be upset—especially after I made a special meal.

I got angrier each time Bill didn't call. As soon as he got home, I either exploded with loud words about how I had worked on his dinner, and he didn't even have the courtesy to call, or I moped around and tried to make him feel guilty. I worked myself into quite a mess before he got home, and then kept it going by letting it out on him. I knew I was angry, and I felt self-righteous. I believed it was fine to be angry. I also believed it was fine to let him know what I was feeling by yelling. I totally believed he *should* call. In my family of origin sarcasm, yelling and blame were the norm. I didn't know any other way to behave and the issue came up repeatedly for years.

While Bill and I attended our first relationship class, I became aware of other possibilities of behavior. I was amazed by how much better I felt being responsible about changing my behavior. I learned to modify my response when he came home late without calling. I would just be quiet, still angry, but not wanting to put it on him. I now understood my reaction was my Responsibility (100%). He could consider my preparing a meal for him and call, or not. I could still want him to call, but if he didn't call, that did not give me permission to dump my anger on him.

Giving myself permission to yell at my husband when he walked in late pushed him away from me just when I wanted him to be more loving. I got physically upset as well; the gut and throat got tight, the shoulders hurt. I was still frustrated about the lack of communication, yet making him feel guilty, and pushing him away as he walked in the door, clearly wasn't what I really wanted to do. It wasn't easy for me to stop expressing my frustration with blame and yelling. Yet, when I fully understood that I was yelling at Bill to make him feel guilty, it became easier to not yell when he came home late without calling.

Being left with my anger instead of dumping it on Bill, I felt the force of the feelings in the body. Over time, I became curious about the mistaken belief behind the anger, which was still there. I recognized the surface belief behind my blind spot was "Bill didn't behave the way I thought he should." That part was easy. However, I still believed he should behave the way I wanted! So the anger continued to live inside my blind spot until I found another important aspect of the truth; "*I* didn't behave the way *I* wanted, dumping my anger or moping around trying to make him feel guilty."

Some television history and more

As my skill with Awareness grew, a healthy distance from my past grew as well. My clarity grew and I was able to understand more of my collection of mistaken beliefs. I discovered other mistaken beliefs feeding my anger. My childhood television shows were *Father Knows Best*, *Ozzie and Harriet*, *Leave it to Beaver*, and *The Donna Reed Show*. These television shows had been absorbed into my unconscious about how family life should be when I grew up. I believed in the happy, vacuous, fictional models portrayed on television because I didn't know any better. When I finally realized the absolute fiction I had been measuring my married life against, I had to laugh.

What Gets in the Way

I sometimes felt betrayed too. Betrayal is the natural consequence of feelings created by our strong attachment to unexplored beliefs. The stronger our attachment to beliefs about marriage, for example, the stronger our sense of betrayal if someone acts differently than we want them to act.

Marriage, for one person, may mean that their partner will take care of their own dinner when they are going to be late and don't call. At the time, my mistaken view of marriage meant that if Bill called when he was going to be late, we had a good marriage. When he didn't call, he betrayed our marriage vows! There is no in-between, no healthy distance, when a person feels betrayed.

I wanted Bill to understand my definition of marriage, and agree with me, even if we had never talked about it. I wanted him to have the same definition without necessarily telling him what I was thinking, and when he didn't, I felt betrayed. I wanted Bill to express his love to me the way I wanted love expressed to me, and when he didn't, I felt betrayed. What a mess!

One day, in a loving moment, we talked about the issue so that I felt heard. Bill was open to a fresh perspective and his blind spot disappeared. He was able to understand my feelings about dinner and communication, and was willing to call when he knew he was going to be late. I'm grateful that years later, he's still good at remembering.

My ability to explore my sense of betrayal came years after Bill began calling when he was going to be late. After I explored the fictional beliefs feeding the feelings of betrayal, I was able to forgive Bill fully. Sometimes we are so caught up in strongly held mistaken beliefs it is *only* on reflection that we can maintain enough healthy distance to glean the wisdom of our experience. Exploring our pain-producing beliefs is exactly what we need to do in order to develop a healthy distance, so that we can feel strong feelings, and not act on them.

Living with another person can often be difficult because we each bring our own full backpack of mistaken beliefs into the shared living space. It can take a long time to unravel our confusion and, at times, it can be difficult, challenging, and intensely uncomfortable. Bill and I have had a long journey together and we have both remained committed to our personal growth and relationship throughout. Each of us has experienced times of remembering and forgetting our commitment to personal growth. There can be long spaces of time in the forgetting phases.

Perhaps our personal story can serve to help the reader have more patience with their partner, realizing that relationship gardens need considerable care. We can take a lifetime to work out our confusion together. Each person has to do his or her part in order for a relationship to work well. Creating loving relationships is a work in progress.

Loving enough to let others be

Getting caught up in wanting people we love to be different feels familiar, doesn't it? It is so easy to see how other people should be different; how they should be happier or more responsible. Have you noticed how trying to convince a partner that she should change, seems to just push her in the opposite direction? When she isn't asking for help, pointing out her blind spot doesn't

What Gets in the Way

help. Yet, we still want to be helpful, don't we? What can be done? The Zen teacher, Norman Fischer[20] reminds us:

> "You can't point out people's blind spots to them.
> If they weren't blind spots you could,
> but since they are blind spots
> they won't see them.
> So it is better to just be loving.
> When they are ready to see through the blind spot they will."

In our family story, I continued to love Bill, and explore my own blind spots. He felt safe enough to finally hear me because I had focused on my own issues and continued to love him. Even though it took years for that to happen, the wait was worth it. Telling him what I thought he should do, yelling, or crying certainly didn't work.

First, I had to act on taking Responsibility for my confusion and see through *my* blind spot. I had to learn about my attachment to a false belief about marriage based on fictional television shows. I had to reach an inner peace about him not calling. Then there was space for my loving him as he walked in the door. Being more loving when he came home late without calling, even though I still felt a little upset, he had the emotional space he needed to notice *his* blind spot. He was open as we finally talked calmly, and he changed. It is the

---

[20] Fischer, Norman, retrieved from Everyday Zen, December 11, 2005.
Web Site:http://www.everydayzen.org/teachings/talk_mumonkan13.asp

way things can work because we are willing to explore our blind spots, go deeper, and find out what's true.

Who in your life do you wish would behave differently? What can you do to be more loving?

More about Naming Practice

As our understanding deepens, we become aware of repetitive pain-producing reactions. Naming Practice[21] helps us explore different mind states—such as "Poor Me," "Self-Judgment," "Right and Wrong" and "Pass and Fail"— when we are caught up in them. Recognizing and naming our confused mind state—or feelings like anger, frustration, jealousy, impatience—we are healthfully thinking and feeling. Having been temporarily caught up in our reactivity, Naming Practice opens a healthy distance so we can mindfully explore the cause. Going deeper, Naming Practice can be an integral part of our blossoming.

Helpful experience and information

For those who have a difficult time understanding what they are feeling, certain experiences can help fill in the gaps. Psychotherapy, workshops focusing on inner reflection, and spiritual guidance with a meditation teacher can be useful when we want to understand the stories behind our feelings. Reading can provide useful information on learning about feelings, too. It can be especially useful to read about biological/emotional differences between men and women. Correct information is essential. Yet, ultimately, we need to experience our feelings

---

[21] See page 78 for additional information about Naming Practice.

and explore mistaken beliefs with Awareness, to integrate new information into our understanding and live with more wisdom.

Activities which foster body/mind connections help us touch directly into the body's experiences. Meditation, yoga, therapeutic massage, Rubenfeld Synergy Method, Qi Gong, Alexander Technique, Feldenkrais Method, and T'ai chi are some of the many useful body/mind experiences available to us.[22] Through deepening our relationship with the body/mind, we learn what it is to have a quieter mind, and to be with the body in a new way.

It is critical to understand that it is our attachment to our unexamined beliefs that causes the pain in our relationships. When we "get it," a genuine heart-felt Curiosity arises. Curiosity carries us along so that we can recognize our confusion and our contribution to the confusion of others. Activated Curiosity focuses our attention on finding out what is true.

A desire to know *what's going on* is essential. Beliefs of all kinds can be explored freshly when we notice the body's message system telling us to Stop, Look, and Listen because something doesn't *feel right*. Discomfort goes from being a disconnected, unquestioned, unpleasant occurrence to our direct connection with a personal mystery longing to be solved.

Over time, we can become so familiar with the body's message system that the open, unfettered, loving experience we have when we know what's true becomes the measure of how we live and love. Recognizing any aspect of our story, and even our whole story, as it arises, we can notice it and let it pass

---

[22] Please keep in mind that suggestions of practices or therapeutic modalities are based on my personal experiences only. Any class, book, or therapeutic experience that draws your attention, feels right, and offers the opportunity for going deeper can be helpful.

through the body/mind. Then our understanding has deepened enough to experience our flowering directly. We can *know* the difference for ourselves between what's true and what isn't true through our connection with the body's message system.

3. Thoughts as visitors

It is useful to understand thought as a visitor, in exploring pain-producing beliefs. Thoughts, just like visitors, come and go. Like greeting a visitor, we can be welcoming. Awareness is a perpetually open door whether we understand it or not. Intrinsically, we have the freedom to respond freshly, welcoming *what is*, with openness. As we come to understand the true nature of thought, we notice the pain-producing thought-visitor, and find freedom by not blindly reacting.

Responding to our thoughts as visitors, we are using skills for mindfulness. We are practicing being more aware. There are two basic aspects of Awareness practice. One aspect is the ability to be mindful, to focus and pay attention. We develop our focus "muscle," just as we exercise at the gym and build specific muscles. The more we use it, the stronger it gets. Our strengthened focus muscle lets us stay on one channel, instead of frantically clicking the remote of our life.

The other aspect is presence, or being with *what is*. Presence is the spaciousness we experience, as we let thoughts and sensations pass through the body/mind without getting caught up in them. The more we cultivate Awareness the more presence becomes our normal way of being. Focus and presence can be talked about separately, yet both are intertwined. And both are essential for identifying our pain-producing thought-visitors.

Focus and Awareness

Awareness Meditation helps us practice staying focused and being more present. Over time, our thought patterns change. Practicing being aware and curious during meditation, we find it is easier to discern thoughts. We experience more Awareness in our daily, busy life. One experience informs the other, and as the results become tangible, we know we are on the right path. We become more aware of our thoughts, and begin to have more patience, more Compassion, Awareness, and Energy during the day. We live with more awareness, and naturally wish no harm to the self or others. We may even sleep better. We pay attention to discomfort differently, so that we are more willing to make changes when things don't feel right.

Sitting quietly with an Awareness practice, we experience the coming and going of thought. No one has to tell us about it because we experience it for our self. We notice our thoughts quieting down. In addition, we develop self-discipline and the ability to fully focus our attention for longer periods of time.

We find that focusing on one thing at a time during the day also quiets the mind, whether it is washing dishes, making the bed, talking on the phone, or brushing our teeth. Even when all we have to do is wait for someone, we can focus on our breath and quiet down the body/mind. Some people find it useful to focus within and say "just this" whenever they want to be aware in the present moment.

With practice, we learn how the body/mind informs us. We more easily sense messages from our internal and external environment. If we become tense, we can sense it happening, and pause. And then remember to let sensations pass through the body. We learn about being present.

A lipstick story

Judy was a client who lived with formidable family difficulties everyday. She came to me "hoping for some understanding and guidance" with her issues.

Judy's life was in such chaos she felt she was getting a stomach ulcer. Her parents were in a nursing home and her marriage was in trouble. There were countless issues with her many siblings and relatives. She wasn't talking to her mother-in-law, her husband, or a cousin. When I asked Judy to rate her emotional pain on a scale of 1-10, she said, "Ten." She had tried hypnosis, various energy healing practices, acupuncture, and marriage guidance. They all helped relieve her stress, and boost her confidence temporarily, but Judy's pain and confusion continued to overwhelm her as she dealt with the logistics of day-to-day life.

One day, the simmering volcano of Judy's life erupted while sorting laundry. She found lipstick on her husband's underwear. Judy confronted her husband about it, and he denied it. She didn't believe him and felt furious.

Every week, Judy and I met for our guidance session on a bench alongside a lovely canal path. One day, Judy looked very upset as she walked towards our bench to begin the session. She subtly pointed out a woman sitting on a nearby bench. "There is the woman my husband is having an affair with!" Judy said. She wasn't absolutely sure, but sure enough to make her heart race and face flush. Judy felt the woman had come to spy on her: maybe even sent by her husband. I didn't know if Judy's impression was true, but I knew she was upset.

What Gets in the Way

I suggested we sit in silence together allowing the whole mess of confusing thoughts and feelings to *be*.

We placed our feet on the ground, lowered our eyes to facilitate focusing inward, and sat in silence together. During our sitting the woman left. Afterwards, Judy reported that she had been able to allow the racing, upset thoughts to pass through the mind. She found a fresh perspective and more of a sense of freedom from emotional turmoil. The woman's presence had been a gift and Judy realized that gift.

Judy began to make meditation and Awareness more a part of her life, and she reported feeling much better. "I'm not letting people bother me so much. I take it lighter. I realize other people's stuff is their own and I don't take it so personally. I'm accepting people more for who they are."

Judy's family life continued to be stressful, so our work repeatedly returned to the idea of being aware like "stillness in the midst of a hurricane." She developed her ability to be aware to a point where she wasn't trying to make people behave differently. She initiated relationship work with her husband. She still thought her husband was unfaithful and counseling did not change his denial. She had to accept that she may never know the truth. Judy began to talk with everyone in her family. She was laughing more with her children and reporting enjoying silence when she meditated. Judy said, "I also feel the presence of God, the Divine, or universal Energy within my heart."

Judy continued, "Meditation should be a part of everyone's life. It frees you from all the junk that life gives you or you allow yourself to take. The mind is a very powerful machine. With meditation I see much clearer and life is much gentler." The people in Judy's family didn't change. Judy did. Her painful, uncomfortable life, coupled with a deeply felt desire for honesty, clarity, and Compassion brought Judy to meditation and Awareness. It was worth the work!

Being aware and feeling at the same time

For most of us, being aware and feeling at the same time depends on whether we grew up interacting with people who modeled it. When we are very young, strong feelings can be overwhelming. They have to be expressed and accepted in a loving atmosphere, if we are to know how to be with feelings healthfully. If a trusted adult can be aware with feelings, models consistently, and knows how to guide us, they pass on their understanding in a loving way and we learn it. We realize we can be angry and not hurt our self or others. We realize we can have a hurt toe and still do our homework. We learn to say thank you or no thank you because our feelings send clear messages about what is loving, and what is not. Growing older, we learn that we can feel strongly, disagree with another, and yet remain open to discussion. All this happens with Awareness. We can have our feelings and they don't have to *have* us!

As our understanding deepens, and challenges grow, we refine our skills. Being aware with feeling means we can experience even strong feelings, and remain present. It means we can feel hurt and explore the cause of distress. We can ask for help when we need it. It means that strong physical/emotional sensations, good or painful, are part of *what is*. We can feel our feelings and also allow the bigger picture on our 3-D screen of Awareness.

What Gets in the Way

Not getting lost in sensations created by sad or angry thoughts, we can explore the body's response with Awareness. Try this experiment next time you are aware of feeling sad or being angry. Focus on the physical sensations. Stand still, or sit alone, and study what's happening in the body/mind. The idea is to find something interesting in the exploration. Let the physical sensations be felt without naming them, directing them, or reacting to them. One time it may be easy for you to follow the physical sensations. Another time you may get only a glimmer of noticing openness, before your automatic thinking pilot is engaged. After each time, take note of how you feel, and whether there have been any shifts in your feelings and/or perspective.

We can be present and feel at the same time because Awareness includes feelings. Noticing our thoughts and sensations, including the five senses, all coming and going, happens with Awareness. On just the physical level, the five senses can be extremely challenging because they grab our attention with such immediacy. We also have seemingly instinctive tastes for what we like and don't like when it comes to our senses. Attachment to our preferences keeps us entangled in our past. Being unattached to the pleasant and unpleasant, allows us to move through life with more Awareness.

It's easy to remember the fullness of pleasant sensory experiences. However, taste, sight, sound, touch, and smell, offer a marvelous opportunity for experiencing unpleasantness with Awareness, as well. For instance, we can taste medicine that tastes awful, and take it anyway. Or, we can smell the unpleasant odor of a sick loved one, and hug them. Sitting in close quarters with young children, we might smell intestinal gas and remain quiet about it, to not embarrass a child. We may not like listening to hard rock music, but when our teenage son is excited about meaningful lyrics of a rock song, we may listen differently for him.

However, being aware and feeling at the same time can seem far-fetched to someone like Tina, who at age twenty-eight, had never heard of it. She rolled her eyes, and laughed. "That is preposterous!" Tina had gotten lost in the sensations of her emotions all her life. She let unconscious thought rule the moment, without Curiosity or Awareness. Tina felt she had to express every thought or feeling in order to feel alive. Now, with more Awareness, she is beginning to learn to discern feelings and thought, and unravel her mistaken belief that feelings have to be all-consuming events.

As she continues to explore being aware and feeling at the same time, Tina now giggles as she remembers her initial response to the idea. After a lifetime of being carried away with feelings, she is beginning to realize another possibility.

Can you remember a time when you were aware and feeling at the same time? What happened? How does the body feel in the remembering? Just notice whatever comes up. There's no right or wrong way to feel.

No-Thought Experiences

Most of us can remember a situation when we acted with total immediacy, our senses and intelligence on high alert. Perhaps it was an emergency, or a time when we took action selflessly, without fear. People often wonder about these moments, and dwell on the clarity they felt and the absolute rightness of action. Even though terrible things may have happened, or nearly happened, the memory of the time feels full because there was a coming together of clarity, action, and compassionate response.

My mother told the story, countless times, of the night I put my head of short curly hair too near the Chanukah candles, and my hair caught on fire. She walked quickly and calmly to the sink, wet a dishcloth, and covered my head. The story and her clear response played in her mind over and over, because there was no thought, no fear, only loving action. I imagine, because she suffered from schizophrenia, that the clarity of her response felt wondrous to her, especially in contrast to her daily mind, often filled with fears and confusion.

In that moment my mother was a hero. Interestingly, the people we call heroes, also describe the absolute clarity and selflessness they feel when caught in a time of crisis. They say they just do the only thing they *can* do. They act with clear knowing.

Mothers, fathers, athletes, artists, business people, and trades people; anyone deeply involved in his or her work, experiences "no thought" when they are fully engaged. Mindfulness practice and meditation help us cultivate this ability of moment-to-moment Awareness, even at the dinner table. It is sometimes called Flow, or being in the Zone. In Zen it is called being "at one" with *what is*. It is worth the practice.

It's up to us

Life can be painful. Whenever we notice we are stuck on a conveyor belt, going round and round with the same painful issues arising again and again, we can be sure that there is at least one belief keeping the motor running so we can't get

What Gets in the Way

off. We have to be willing to explore our underlying beliefs, even though that part of our adventure is scary, and the outcome is unknown. The alternative, an endless ride on the conveyor belt of suffering from our confusion, is not a healthy choice.

Exploring our thoughts and feelings with Awareness makes this alternative way of living come alive. We can let our Longing for more love and clarity take us to new understanding and full flowering of our being. Wondering about what beliefs are in the way of our relationships, leads us to be more present. We also need to keep our sense of Humor and be willing to explore the unknown. Even though it can be scary.

Chapter Four

Fear as Fertilizer

Feel the fear and read this anyway

This chapter explores how fear gets in the way of our being who we long to be, and who we really are. We also discover how fears can help us become our unique expression of the Flowering of Inner Growth. This chapter might be challenging to read. For some people, just reading the word "fear" can create uncomfortable sensations that feel so overpowering they can't focus on reading.[23]

If you feel uncomfortable, take a few moments to notice what's happening in the body without labeling sensations. Allow the sensations to be, and stay with them, bringing Curiosity to them. Where are they? What is happening? Do they shift? Where are they moving? Is there stillness also? When you are more comfortable, continue.

We may need professional help addressing some fears, and that's okay. Also, we may not address every fear in this lifetime. We usually deal with certain fears first; the fears that get in the way of relationships or jobs we care deeply about.

Think about something you recently avoided: calling for support, approaching a family member about a painful situation, or writing a letter that has been sitting in your file for months. Usually, when we imagine something difficult, we experience resistance. We instinctively avoid pain in any form.

---

[23]Some people may not feel ready for this direct approach to being with fear. There has to be a readiness, and often a direct relationship with an experienced teacher to help us deal with some of our deeper fears. And there may be a time in our practice for psychotherapy even when we have a teacher.

What Gets in the Way

We may procrastinate. We may feel tightening in the chest, butterflies in the stomach, or a dry throat. We often label these sensations as "fear" and avoid going anywhere near whatever caused those feelings in the first place.

If we see our lives as either moving *toward* fear or *with* love, then Balance is the place where we can acknowledge fears as they arise, and not let them control us. Our response to fear can keep us from living a joyful, awake life. Feeding our fear, we avoid, deny, and ignore *what is*. Feeling our fear, we can acknowledge, explore, and be with *what is*.

There are many unexplored fears that bubble beneath the surface. When we are afraid, we might not get to know a new person, go to the doctor, take a yoga class, study our financial situation, or call a friend who can help us— even though these actions may bring us more intimacy, health, clarity, and happiness.

Seeking a healthier life usually means we need to step outside our comfort zone, in spite of how difficult it feels. In order to overcome a fear, such as going to the dentist, picking up the phone when we are waiting to hear about a job, hiring a business coach, or trying anything new, we need to feel the fear and do it anyway, even when that means taking baby-step-by-baby-steps.

We must be willing to explore our fears even though the exploration can be challenging and uncomfortable. Recently, my friend Steve shared a story about Inge, a woman he knows who makes $55,000/year and believes that she will end up on the streets as a bag lady when she grows old. Inge doesn't know for certain what will happen. Yet her fear about the future feels so real to her that she allows it to be in the way of her generosity and caring for herself and others in the present.

What Gets in the Way

Unless Inge is willing to step out of her comfort zone and question her fears about the future, she will continue to let her unconscious beliefs affect her life.

1. Everyday Fears

What is fear anyway? Does it always get in the way? And does it always have to be so *bad*? It has been said that fear was put into our body/mind system as a form of protection. The limbic area of the brain takes charge when our survival is threatened. The sympathetic nervous system gets turned on. This is commonly called the "fight or flight response." If we are walking down a dark alley at night and hear footsteps from behind, fear is the trigger that puts the body on alert. Adrenalin surges through our veins. In case of attack, fear engages the whole body in the protection of life. It is a survival instinct. If we are trained in martial arts, or another form of self-defense, our body/mind responds from our training. Though for most of us, we just do what we can to survive. We may run, fight back, or surrender. We are experiencing a survival moment and that is enough. We are in the moment and we act, one way or another.

After a fearful event, we often replay the incident. We think about what we might have done differently. Perhaps our pain-producing belief system kicks in and we judge our self. Upset stomach, nausea, tears may arise again, remembering the incident. We may even turn to blame and hatred, wanting revenge on whoever hurt or scared us.

Everyday life brings us opportunities to be with non-life threatening fears created by our unexamined thoughts: the first day on a new job, an elderly parent being ill, "losing" the car in a parking lot, our son going out with a group of boys we don't know, a daughter going out on her first date and coming home late. There is plenty of fertilizer to work with when we want to be with our everyday fear in a way that is useful, honest, and loving. And it is not easy.

What is this, really?

It's important to question beliefs that create fear in our life, by asking, "What is this, really?" Fears may be on the surface and easily seen. They may be accessible with self-inquiry or remain unconscious. It generally takes work to see how much we let fear rule our life. Unless we are curious, we won't see what's true. Being aware helps because we become familiar with the body's response to conscious or unconscious fearful thought.

Fear thoughts tend to develop into whole stories that affect how we do things, and what we don't do. We may feel uncomfortable going to a picnic with new people. Noticing the discomfort, acknowledging our fear, we can still go. We may be afraid to speak in front of a group, and stand up and do it. If we are uncomfortable in a new situation and decide to stay home, or call in at the last minute to cancel a speaking engagement, we may not be aware that fear is controlling us. We may have a whole list of justifications, e.g. "Everyone in my family is the same way," or "I wouldn't like anyone who's there anyway." Noticing something in the way of becoming who we long to be, we can bring awareness to our discomfort, engage Curiosity, and explore it.

If you feel overwhelmed by all this information about fear, try this. Be with the breath for a moment or two. Bring Awareness to your sensations for a while. Now keep reading. After all, Awareness is what this book is about.

What Gets in the Way

A lost child

I learned something about fear one day, when our son was very young. It was a beautiful spring day and Jason was outside playing. He always stayed right in front of the house where I could see him from my window. But, this time when I looked, he was gone!

Fear of what might have happened to him gripped me. I had no faith, only fear. Mother-worry took over. As seconds grew to minutes and the minutes grew into what seemed like hours, I became frantic. In the end he was gone just two hours, but it seemed like an eternity at the time.

It was long enough for me to call the police, for them to come with dogs, look inside our couch, and then stand around outside deciding how to organize a search of the ravine surrounding our home. It was hell. My life was completely, terribly, on hold.

I remember we were at the top of our driveway with the dogs, intensely discussing what to do next, when I looked up and noticed our son standing next to a neighbor who was watching on the outer edges of all this excitement. Jason was watching, too!

It was an amazing moment! Where had he been for two hours? He had been upstairs at our neighbor's. Their door was left open and he had walked right in and went upstairs to play in their daughter's room. No one had seen him go in.

Such complete relief…then thoughts of embarrassment. I had called the police… self-blaming thoughts, "What did I do wrong?" "I should have been watching him better…" And blaming, "He should have stayed where he was supposed to stay."

143

I called to Jason, grabbed him, and held him tightly. And then I cried. He had no idea what was going on, yet he sensed my need to hold him. It took me months to get over that day. Thoughts of losing Jason again played over and over. I watched him more closely and didn't let him out of my sight for a long time. All parents know that the line between fear and raising a child with some degree of equanimity can be very thin!

Jason was, in fact, missing. However, it was also true that thoughts of the worst possible outcome grabbed me completely. It was possible that he was lost in the woods, and it turned out he wasn't. He might've been kidnapped. Fear of what might've happened kept my attention and adrenalin going. Fear in such circumstances is understandable and simply part of the parenting job.

Even when we lose Awareness in the midst of a scary experience, Awareness helps us recover more easily. When we are aware, we can recognize mistaken fears, be grateful for a good outcome, and get on with life. At the end of that day, fortunately, all my scary thoughts proved to be False Evidence Appearing Real.

False Evidence Appearing Real

An acronym that can be helpful as fear arises is FEAR, or False Evidence Appearing Real. Beneath everyday fears are beliefs about what we don't know, yet so readily believe. There are so many interdependent unknown variables affecting all that happens. We can never know exactly what will happen to us in the next moment, let alone the distant future. With Awareness, we become more comfortable with not knowing how things will work out. Letting fears come and go; we stay open and present with *what is*.

Every kind of prejudice is a kind of fear based on our false interpretation of limited evidence. Statistics, politics, movies, and newspapers often support our fears by providing information in ways that make false or limited evidence appear real. Yet when we step out of our comfort zone, and explore for our self what's true, we learn how false and limiting our fears can be.

2. Learning From Fear

Feeling and not reacting

We instinctively avoid situations, and people, that trigger our fear reactions. Powerful sensations can be triggered by the mistaken beliefs making up our stories. If we are to understand what stimulates our fear reactions, we need to bring our Curiosity and Awareness to the situation. With gentle care, we can be present with the discomfort. Feeling ready to experience strong feelings and work on *not reacting*, we find new ways to help us untangle our fears and the beliefs that sustain them.

Most of us have different ways of modifying our behavior to handle fears. If we didn't, we would be too afraid to get out of bed in the morning. We may have a scary meeting with a colleague, yet we can feel what's happening internally, and still go to the meeting. We may feel our stomach doing turns, and make that first phone call to find out about a new class we've been considering. We can feel internal chaotic sensations and still pick up the phone and explore changing jobs.

Although we may unconsciously handle fears every day, Awareness offers freedom on a whole new level. Between feeling the fear and not reacting, there is a space where our Creativity can move us in healthy ways. Being present, we can feel uncomfortable, creative, and completely alive at the same time.

Awareness helps us acknowledge the presence of fear without letting fearful thoughts run our life. Imagine playfully thinking of fearful thoughts as "little beings" attracted to Awareness for love and healing. Greeting fearful thoughts with a simple, "No, thank you." is one way to embrace fear with Awareness. We can learn to be more loving, even with fear thoughts!

Fears can make us Stop, Look, and Listen

Experiencing a strong physical/emotional discomfort or even a twinge, we can recognize it as a Stop sign. Remember the childhood lesson, Stop, Look, and Listen? It can still be used as an Awareness tool: stopping what we're doing, looking inside, and listening, by bringing Curiosity and Awareness to the situation. Then, we listen not only with ears, but also with the whole body/mind system. We Stop-Look-Listen, asking simply, "What is this?"

Intrigued? Here's how it works. First, allow the thought or image to arise of someone you fear or an uncomfortable situation. Be aware of any desire to push away or change the image or thought. Just be curious about what is happening inwardly, without naming your experience. Can you bring the open question, "What is this?" right into the sensation? Notice what happens.

Noticing whatever is going on, without trying to push it away or deny it, or even name it, we experience the sensations as they move through the body system. We are in the moment, fully present to the feelings. We can notice how sensations run through the body and change— not grabbing hold and making them more or less than *what is*. See what this is like for yourself next time you are in fear. See if you can notice, be curious, and not react to what's happening inside.

A personal example

A few years ago, a friend recommended *Loving What Is* by Byron Katie. One Sunday afternoon, I easily immersed myself in the book. After a while, much to my surprise, I found myself standing up next to the chair. Looking down, the book was sitting on the chair. This happened two or three times, before I realized something "weird" was going on. I had no Awareness of how I came to be standing up next to the chair!

I stopped and looked at what was happening. Consciously, attentively, I picked up the book and pinpointed the paragraph I was reading before I jumped up. I "listened" by exploring what had made me put the book down. I quickly discovered the cause of my tremendous resistance. The paragraph mentioned the Nazis' throwing babies onto the trains when they were loading people for the concentration camps. This time, I noticed feeling a great heaviness and deep discomfort in my heart area. I had been so uncomfortable with this horrifying

What Gets in the Way

image that I went into reaction. When I became aware of what had happened, stayed with my feelings, and identified their cause, I could keep reading.

Since the book was about how to explore the kind of reaction I had, now I really wanted to finish it! The material in *Loving What Is* is now an integral part of my guidance work. If I hadn't stayed with uncomfortable feelings and explored *what is*, I wouldn't have discovered Katie's practical, loving work, and the desire to share it with others.[24]

A frightful hike

When Bill and I were newly married, we went on a five day backpacking trip to the Presidential Range in the White Mountains in New Hampshire. I had only been camping and day hiking before, and this was an adventure. I thought I would love it all. But, on our first day out, we faced challenges that proved daunting for me. First, I could barely stand up with my pack, so Bill took more and more of my pack's weight. Then we came to the boulder field that led up to the top of Mt. Madison. I had never seen anything like it.

We started hiking over the boulders, one by one. Bill had gone ahead and, in the beginning, I was doing fine. Then I turned around and looked below. Totally irrational fears of falling down the mountain completely gripped me. I froze.

Bill noticed that I had stopped and came back to check on me. I knew I couldn't go down and was afraid to move. With Bill's kind words of encouragement,

---

[24] For more information about Byron Katie's work see A Short List of Related Reading on page VII at the end of this book.

What Gets in the Way

I made my way up, step by step. At a snail's pace, we made our way to the top. I felt better by the time we got there, but was uncomfortable enough that I still didn't want to look back.

On the second day, the unexpected happened. We had hiked over Mt. Jefferson and Mt. Adams, and it got very cold. The wind picked up enough to make it impossible to cook dinner. A strong wind blew all night across from Mount Washington. We spent one long cold night inside a wind-collapsed tent. We woke up to ice-covered puddles nearby. The wind was so strong that next morning, we had to crawl on our hands and knees to the other side of a pass, where the wind was less fierce. Despite the strong winds and cold, I had made it through once again.

After that, I got better at taking backpacking challenges with less and less fear, as my self-confidence grew. I loved looking out over the fall scenery, growing more colorful each day.

The fourth day, I climbed down ladders precariously nailed into the sides of cliffs, and passed backpacks through spaces between rocks, just big enough for us to crawl through afterwards. In the end, hiking out, I looked back over my shoulder at Mt. Madison and laughed at what now looked like a tiny mound of boulders. My initial, fearful climb was truly behind me, in more ways than one.

I share this experience because fear taught me a big lesson about "keep going" on that trip. I learned to step into unreasonable fears and that is what made me feel stronger at the end of each day.

Think about a time in your life when you were afraid—a time when a fear prevented you from doing what you wanted. Wondering about the

What Gets in the Way

beliefs that created that fear may open the way for you to respond with Awareness next time around.

When dying is *what is*

Late one evening, on my way to a much-needed night's sleep, the phone rang. A woman named Helen introduced herself and apologized for calling so late. When I mentioned I was on my way to bed, she explained, "I was on my way to bed too, but I knew if I didn't call you right now, I never would."

Helen's friend had given her my number several weeks before, yet Helen was afraid to call right away, because she had never called an energy healer. Helen told me she was at the end of her rope and hoped to find a way to make her mother get better. Helen's 78-year old mother had inoperable pancreatic cancer.

Helen was desperate to help her mother "get better." Helen was a physician, trained in St. Petersburg, Russia, and had spent her whole working life "saving" other people. Now her mother was dying and she was trying to save her mother's life. She called me, hoping that Qi Gong would be the miracle she longed for.

Helen described the family struggle in her life. Helen and her father hadn't told her mother what Helen called "the grim prognosis." Her mother was talking a lot more about love than she ever had. Helen did not understand that her mother probably knew she was dying. Her dad kept cooking for his beloved wife, and was constantly frustrated by her not eating what he had prepared. She was not interested in food; she was sleeping much of the day. He was upset about her sleeping so much, because he wanted to spend more time with her. He didn't know that it is normal at the end of life to sleep a lot and lose interest in food.

Helen kept thinking about how healthy and strong her mother had been all her life, before she got sick. She hoped her mom could be like that again someday. Neither Helen, nor her dad, saw the truth right before their eyes because they were holding on to what they *wanted* to be true. They were fighting the inevitable because of their fear.

Helen's mother was dying, and Helen knew intellectually she couldn't prevent death. But this was her mother. Helen didn't want her mother to die. She had never studied the dying process. She did not understand what had been happening to her mother. The pain and confusion Helen felt during her mother's dying process was natural. She was losing a person she loved and would miss deeply. She didn't want her mother to suffer and didn't want her to die. She felt helpless in the face of what she could not prevent—losing her beloved mother. All of these conflicting inner messages created chaos in the body/mind. Fear of the unknown was driving confusion.

Confusion is created by feeding the fear of *what is*. And her confusion was what led Helen to call for help. Perhaps, the struggle in Helen's family quieted down, as each member of the family developed an acceptance of the dying process. They may have learned to be fully present with *what is*, as a beloved mother and wife passed from their life.

Awareness helps us be more comfortable with not knowing, and the reality of physical death. We are better able to be with our fears, and the changes that are inevitable as a person is dying. We can openly express our grief. We can respond to their physical needs. We are more present. Being open to *what is* in the dying process of a loved one, we may be deeply enriched by their dying experience, as well as their life.

Fears help wake us up

Whenever we are curious about what has created our fear—unexplored beliefs about success, failure, death, not being enough, not knowing, kidnapping, heights, drowning, losing a job, flying, or loss of a loved one—we are awake to other possibilities. We are open to change from the *status quo*. Fear-based habits become Stop-Look-Listen moments. Exploring the history of our family situation, we get to know our story in greater depth. The reasons for our belief system become clearer. With more clarity, we can recognize our fears as they get in the way of *what is*. We may try new things. Because fear helps stimulate our healing journey, we can even feel grateful for it. And remember we can seek help— from a meditation teacher, hospice chaplain, family member, minister, priest, friend, or psychotherapist.

Fears remain in the way of our blossoming, unless we do the work of bringing them to light freshly, Stop-Look-Listen, bit by bit, with Compassion, gentleness, and grace.

Chapter Five
Urban Meditator Devours Crocodile and Other Mistaken Ideas about Meditation

Top 12 Myths

You know how some myths are created. A person hears something and expands the story and shares it with others as if it were true. People believe it and question it no further. Just think about the phenomenon of urban myths! If you are new to this form of story telling, go to Google®, type in "urban myths" and you'll find dozens of listings! *Stray Doggie Adopted by Tourists Turns Into a Sewer Rat. Palm Beach Golfer is Devoured by Large Crocodile.*

Although the media hasn't yet reported *Urban Meditator Devours Crocodile*, or *Meditation Causes Hives*, many myths have grown up around meditation. What happens when you say the word *meditation*? In my experience people tend to:

- Look blank.
- Suggest they know all about meditation and it is not for them.
- Say they've already tried and can't sit still.
- Say their thoughts are too busy and they can't do it.

What Gets in the Way

It used to be, when meditation was suggested almost everyone would look blank. Thirty years ago when I first heard about meditation, my initial response was similar. Meditation wasn't "me." I assumed I could never do it. These days, meditation is written about and suggested by everyone from spiritual teachers, to doctors, yoga teachers, talk-show hosts, and basketball coaches. Among the hundreds of modern spiritual masters who have recommended meditation are: His Holiness the Dalai Lama, Pema Chödrön, Thich Nhat Hanh, Toni Packer, Thomas Merton, Steven and Ondrea Levine, Joseph Goldstein, Sylvia Boorstein, Ram Dass, Jack Kornfield, and Jon Kabat-Zinn.

Meditation is believed to have existed since human beings first realized they could be aware of their own mind. Yet many people hear about meditation, read the books, and for one reason or another, decide they can't do it!

Misinformation about meditation and what to expect from it abound. Have you tried meditation and given up, or decided you can't even try? Do you have a reason for not meditating? If so, what is it?

For fun, I've compiled a list of the top myths people say when I ask, "Have you tried to meditate?" Please bring your Curiosity and see if you find yourself on the list. The myths are a fun way to explore attitudes about meditation, and when seen in a new light, they free up the subject so you can find out for yourself. Notice how you greet the information. Check yourself for self-judgment and openness. Try shining your light of Curiosity and sense of Humor into your personal myths.

MYTH 1: Busy Myth

"My mind is too busy; It can't quiet down."

Busy Myth is the biggest myth. It is based on the assumption that people who meditate don't have busy minds, and are more able to concentrate than *I can*.

Thought happens. This is a fact. Thoughts come and go. Everyone has thoughts, including meditation teachers. Sometimes thoughts feel like a continual surge, like a waterfall or an intense action movie. At other times, thought is like small waves lapping on a quiet beach. With practice, we learn to focus inwardly. As we observe how thought works we can get less drawn into the thought content and unconscious reactivity. We may even notice the spaces between thoughts. Our relationship with thought changes with practice. We can notice a thought and wonder, "Where does it come from?" "Is it true?" "How does it relate to my emotional/physical sensations?"

Our minds are often so busy, the ancients called this busy-ness "monkey mind" because monkeys are so active and unpredictable, just like thoughts. We get caught up and behave from our thoughts, although we have no perspective about whether these thoughts are true or not. A good way to learn more about our thoughts is to occasionally notice what kind of thought we are having. Is my thought a loving thought? A fearful thought? A planning thought? A remembering thought?

Different thought experiences

Let's say there are eight different experiences of thought:

What Gets in the Way

1. Loving thoughts; expressing Compassion, empathy, Curiosity, clarity, spiritual practices; including prayer and mantra
2. Fear-based thoughts; expressing judgments, blame, failure, anger, frustration, jealousy, envy
3. Planning thoughts; organizational work, calendars, event planning
4. Remembering thoughts; having a memory without adding to it
5. Informational descriptive thoughts; snowy day, sunny day, thunderstorm, "just this," "I am."
6. Creative thoughts; inspiration
7. Open- ended inquiring thought; Who am I? What is this?
8. No thought; when life occurs spontaneously with no thought present[25]

Awareness helps us become familiar with our thoughts. Curiosity about thought naturally arises as we notice how quickly they pass through, how many there are, and how easily the body reacts to thought, both conscious and unconscious.

Realizing how little control we actually have over "monkey mind" helps to develop a sense of Humor about thought. As our experiences of Awareness increase, we have a healthier relationship with "monkey mind," and can laugh as it jumps from one thought to another, like a monkey swinging from trees. Watch out for those snarley branches—like judgments or blaming thoughts— though, because they sure can get in the way!

---

[25] As soon as we name No thought (#8), it is no longer experienced.

What Gets in the Way

MYTH 2: Control Myth

"I can't stop my thoughts."

Some of us have heard stories about spiritual masters who have quieted all thought. We mistakenly believe we should be able to stop thought by shear force of will. We can't stop our thoughts by fighting them. Whenever we fight thoughts, we keep them alive because we believe that they are real enough to battle.

Thought is simply part of our human experience. With meditation, we can notice thoughts stopping as we are fully focused on the breath. And then they come and go again as we continue practicing. Thoughts will always come and go. In our daily life, with Awareness practice, thoughts can quiet down to a remarkable degree but it doesn't ever happen because we willed them to be still.

Meditation has been used for millennia because it is so effective as a mind training practice. A meditation practice is a highly efficient and practical ongoing experience that helps us be more awake to our thoughts. In the quiet of a meditation experience, we can notice thoughts pass through the mind like clouds pass across the sky. Sometimes the sky is stormy, sometimes clear, and bright. Clouds change their form and move on, without us having to *do* anything to them.

We learn to recognize different kinds of thought clouds. And we can notice getting caught up in a thought that becomes a story holding our attention for a while. Another time we can have enough Awareness to let the thought simply pass through.

Actually, when we stop trying to control thought, and become Curious instead, something interesting may occur. We may notice the space between thoughts. Can you imagine noticing the space between your thoughts? Imagine resting there for a moment or two.

Thought is not bad or good. It just *is*.

MYTH 3: Sitting Still Myth

"I can't sit still. I have to move!"

I can relate to this one. Worries about having to *just sit* can be quite an obstacle. Picture this. It is 1958. It is a hot summer day, a wiggly nine-year-old girl, and her twelve-year-old brother, have been sitting for hours in the back seat of the family sedan as it rolls across the American prairie on summer vacation. No air conditioning, windows wide open. The brother bets his sister she can't sit still, and they get into an argument. Their voices go back and forth. Their mother turns around and bets the little girl she can't sit still, even for one minute. Mom times it on her watch. The little girl tries and tries, but she can't sit still.

I was that little girl in constant motion. When I grew up and got interested in meditating, the body still didn't want to be still. The energies in the body felt so intense, that it took everything I had to feel what I was feeling and stay still. I remember feeling like there were thousands of ants creating havoc inside me.

What made me continue with sitting meditation? Why didn't I just get up and say "To hell with this!" Forward to age twenty-eight. By then, I had been in psychotherapy and understood enough of my family history to have some objectivity. There was more pain in my relationships than I wanted, and I was looking for more help. I found two books that gave me new direction. Shunryu Suzuki's *Zen Mind Beginner's Mind* and Philip Kapleau's *The Three Pillars of Zen*.

What Gets in the Way

Both books made it clear that bodily sensations were part of Awareness and meditation experience. Suzuki Roshi gave me new information about the mind, and helpful information about changing my habits. Roshi Kapleau taught me how to concretely begin a meditation practice with instructions on sitting. If I wanted to have clarity and wisdom, which they assured me was already there, I needed to experience the sensations of the body without *doing* anything about it. So, I sat with my feelings. I sat with the restlessness, the antsy-ness, the aching, and the wanting to get up. And the feelings passed. Whew!

Just as thoughts come and go, physical sensations come and go. Nothing stays the same. Einstein was once asked to put into words the one thing, which summed up *all* he had learned in his lifetime. He reportedly responded, "Something is moving." That means *all* the time!

MYTH 4: Must Be Comfortable Myth

"I can't meditate because it makes me feel uncomfortable."

Coming to meditation with the Intention to relax, our body may do exactly what we want it to do. Meditation for relaxation can be extremely useful in today's stressed world. And yet, what happens if the body doesn't relax? Physical discomfort, like thought, is part of life.[26] It is also a Stop sign that catches our attention quite easily. Discomfort is valuable when we realize the body's messages

---

[26] If you don't want to accept this, I challenge you to find one person who has never felt any physical discomfort.

are signaling a need for gentle attention and careful exploration. Discomfort sends a message to us to wake up and notice something.

Sitting still, and staying with *what is*, physical sensations arise. Muscles tighten, muscles relax, noses itch, feelings come and go, tears form and drop, and sensations arise and subside. The body gives us important clues about how the mind and body work. Refraining from immediately seeking to escape discomfort or perpetuate pleasure, we can be aware, open, curious, and willing to explore what's happening.

For instance, I can stay with the antsyness I sometimes feel, and experience it just as it is, no pulling away, simply noticing with Curiosity what's happening. Thoughts come and go about wishing to feel better, and wanting to move or get up. Often, I notice the sensations change.

The qualities of discomfort are nuanced. It is possible to be with whatever is happening without having to do anything, not even name it. We may even notice when we are quietly, deeply, curious about something, there is no experience of thought. Then we may truly understand what it means to be *open*.

This kind of quiet work with the body's experience helps us deal with our daily life because we are practicing experiencing *what is*. We practice being with the wonderful stuff, without holding on, living it fully, and we remain open for what's next. Practicing being with the uncomfortable stuff, without resistance, we get better at remaining present and balanced in the midst of physical, emotional, mental, and spiritual, challenges we all face—sooner or later.

MYTH 5: Lotus Myth

"I can't meditate because I can't cross my legs into a full lotus posture."

This myth is easy to dispel.[27] You can sit in a chair! Sitting cross-legged, or in full lotus, is not the only way to meditate. There are other postures you can use if sitting on the floor is important to you. People in meditation centers use different shapes and sizes of pillows to support the body in a sitting position. To take the pressure off the knees, you can lift your hips higher with cushions. You can sit in a chair.[28] You can meditate lying down if you like, although there is more of a risk of falling asleep. People also meditate in a standing posture, and when walking. In addition, your comfort level, and the body's ability to take different positions, may change over time.

Whatever meditation posture you take, it is important to have correct alignment. An erect back helps the Energy flow, and allows blood and oxygen to get to the brain more easily than when you are slumped over. If you sit in a chair, make sure your feet are resting on the ground. If the chair is too tall, rest your feet on a book to feel connected to the ground.

Similarly, if you are sitting on a rug, blanket or meditation mat,[29] in a lotus or half lotus, it is best to have the knees in contact with what's beneath you. The knees and buttocks provide a triangular base to physically ground you. You can

---

[27] Meditation is not just about attaining and maintaining a particular posture. It is being with *what is*. Certain meditation postures facilitate our ability to practice. Yet we all have different physical abilities and disabilities and Awareness helps us recognize, and honor them as well.

[28] Yes, I know I already said this, but it bears repeating because so many people think they have to sit on the floor. Sitting on the floor, with cushions properly supporting the body, can help us feel more grounded, yet many people feel chairs work just fine.

[29] It is generally not recommended to sit on a bed for two reasons: 1) Being on a bed usually connotes going to sleep. 2) Many beds are too soft to provide proper support for the lower back.

also sit on a meditation bench or pillow, with your knees close together and your legs folded beneath you.

If you go to Google® and search "meditation postures," you will find many illustrated positions to try out. It is helpful to get one-on-one advice from an experienced meditation, Alexander, or yoga teacher.

Most meditation centers intersperse rounds of sitting with rounds of walking meditation. The longest sitting rounds I've heard of are 60 minutes long, with 15 minutes of walking meditation in between each 60-minute period of sitting. Our meditation group sits for 25 minutes, with a minute or two to stretch in between two rounds, or five minutes of walking—depending on how big the group and the size of the space we're in. Walking meditation is a profound form of meditation because we are practicing Awareness in motion. Since we are in motion much of our life, it is good to practice walking with Awareness. Practicing both walking and sitting meditation is highly recommended.

MYTH 6: Monk (Nun) Myth

"You have to be a monk or nun to have a real meditation practice."

You don't have to leave the everyday world and enter a monastery or meditation center to have a meditation practice. Meditation gives its greatest rewards in the middle of a busy stress-filled life. Many, who spend years away from the world in monasteries and meditation centers, eventually test their understanding and Compassion in everyday life, right in the middle of work and family. The famous ox-herding pictures of Zen beautifully illustrate the return to the marketplace, after the silence of the mountaintop.

What Gets in the Way

Jennifer and Maddy

Here's a real life example of how a woman, who is not a nun, used her meditation practice in the midst of the most challenging family circumstances. A few years ago, I visited, Maddy, an eight year-old girl, who was seriously ill with liver cancer. Two years before, when no one was at home, her father destroyed the inside of their home and killed himself with a shotgun. Within four months, Maddy, then six, developed liver cancer. Maddy's older sister, 11, moved in with grandparents while her mother, Jennifer, and Maddy spent four months in the hospital for Maddy's cancer treatment. The cancer went into remission for a while, but the cancer came back. Jennifer knew that it was likely that Maddy would die.

Together we practiced Qi Gong in her tiny hospital room. Maddy's mother, Jennifer, 34, was constantly by Maddy's side. For weeks Jennifer slept on a chair-bed next to Maddy's hospital bed. Occasionally she went to the cafeteria, but mainly Jennifer stayed close to Maddy, doing everything she could for her daughter.

Jennifer began to meditate while in the hospital. Jennifer was living Awareness every moment. She barely got an hour of straight sleep most nights. Day and night Jennifer was there to help quench Maddy's insatiable thirst. When Maddy said she was thirsty, Jennifer got Maddy something to drink. After each sip of liquid, Jennifer waited patiently for Maddy to signal her to empty the contents of her stomach, using a syringe fitted to a tube hanging out of Maddy's stomach. Then she took Maddy to the toilet.

Maddy slept better during the day, but Jennifer stayed awake to watch over things because the hospital was a training hospital and some of the residents were new. Jennifer knew more about Maddy's history and the cycle of the IV's and medications than some of the nurses and doctors. All day she was alert to every possibility to get the best care for her daughter. And all day and night she tended to Maddy's physical needs as well.

You'd think Jennifer would have collapsed from the strain. Yet, her strength was the amazing thing. Many visitors mentioned a feeling of love, and a presence of clarity and Compassion in the room.

Late one night, a particularly noisy, flashlight-bearing nurse awakened Jennifer. It was one more stress than Jennifer could take. She told me that for a moment she thought, "I can't handle this anymore." Her head pounded and her body felt beyond its limits with sleep deprivation and physical exhaustion. She felt absolute fury arising towards the nurse. But, instead of getting into it, something from Jennifer's meditation practice came to her. She had a glimmer of Awareness that she didn't want to *go there*. The feeling of righteous fury dissipated. She lay down again on her chair bed, meditated, and fell asleep, at least for an hour!

Maddy and her family were in their second round of a long hospital stay within two years, and no one knew when it would end. Jennifer amazed everyone who noticed. She was calm, attentive, loving, and compassionate. With her loving Intentions, and now her meditation practice, Jennifer had gleaned enough clarity and wisdom to help other parents in similar situations. Parents whose children were also hospitalized stopped by Maddy's room to ask Jennifer about hospital life, and share their frustrations and fears. In turn, Jennifer had much to share with them. She was right in the thick of life, in a situation most would imagine unbearable, and she was practicing meditation. Jennifer longed to feel balanced in the midst of chaos. She meditated because it was helpful.

Awareness does not just belong to people who commit their lives to being a monk or a nun. Each time any of us bring one moment of clarity to a chaotic situation at work, one peaceful response in the face of violence on the street, one compassionate word in response to an angry teenager, or a kind, honest remark in the midst of any confusion, we help heal the craziness of our lives and the world. Do you remember a time when a difficult situation eased up because someone responded with honesty, good Humor, or Compassion? What was your experience of the situation? Did you realize how much presence of mind the person showed, by helping things open up for the better? This is why it is so important to become more aware in our chaotic world. As with Jennifer, our Awareness has a profound effect on others. It changes the world for the better, no matter how much pain is present within us and around us.

MYTH 7: Time Myth

"You need loads of spare time in order to meditate."

Here's what people do who understand the value of meditation. They make the time. They get up 10-60 minutes earlier in the morning to sit. They meditate in the evening, while the young ones are falling asleep. My husband and I often sat quietly in our daughter Emily's room, after reading time was over. She would drift off to sleep in the peaceful atmosphere of our quiet Awareness practice.

Many busy people interested in meditation choose to attend short retreats, from a weekend to ten days. They often choose a meditation retreat over a vacation because they feel deeply refreshed after a retreat. Matt, a 55-year old writer told me he discovered years ago that he often felt like he needed a vacation *after* a vacation! A meditation retreat is quite different for Matt. He returns to his life with a powerful source of Energy to fuel his daily life and a fresh perspective to share with his loved ones.

MYTH 8: Other People Myth

"Only special (better, smarter, more loving) people meditate."

For centuries people have been saying that meditation is essential to mental health. Meditation is not new and it is not something for "special people." What beliefs could keep you from sitting down and simply breathing for a few minutes? Bring Curiosity to your long held beliefs and find out what your resistance is really about.

I remember thinking I could never meditate when I first learned about Zen meditation from my boyfriend, now husband, Bill. He had begun a Zen meditation practice months before we got together. I *thought* he was special and better than me because he meditated and practiced Zen. I was in psychotherapy at the time, and knew he must be "more together" than me. I was figuring out my messy relationships with my dad and mom, and couldn't see past my pain to even consider meditation as an option. It wasn't for me, only for people better than me.

After a few intense months of psychotherapy, I had gained a healthier perspective about my relationship with my parents. I had faced the pain from their divorce. I understood the part of me that had felt both fear and relief when

What Gets in the Way

I heard my mother going through the medicine cabinet the night my dad left. I assumed she was looking for some way to commit suicide and did nothing to stop her. I was afraid of how my life would change if I woke up in the morning and found her dead. At the same time, I didn't even think I should stop her. I was so confused that part of me also hoped she would succeed because life with her had been so emotionally painful. I was exhausted from her crying in my arms every night. I hated feeling responsible for her. Now, nearly ten years later, I was beginning to feel free from the feelings that had haunted me and I began to wonder what was next after therapy.

One night, when Bill was out, I reached for *The Three Pillars of Zen* and began to read. I had already read *Zen Mind Beginner's Mind*, but I had never read clear instructions on how to meditate. Here was what I was looking for! I sat down and began counting my breath. It was no longer about other people and not me. All excuses fell away when I was ready.

MYTH 9: Space Myth

"You've got to have a meditation room to meditate."

Even if all you have is a chair, meditation can happen. Since we can meditate walking or standing, all we need is a sidewalk, road, or a closet! Just kidding. You may not want to sit in a closet, although I've had friends who have created a special place no bigger than a closet. You don't need a big space. You can create a sense of sanctuary in the corner of a room. Place your meditation chair or cushion in its own special place to help you remember to sit down and breath with Awareness. In a real sense, all the space you need is the space of your own body/mind.

MYTH 10: Religious Myth

"You have to be Buddhist to meditate."

Meditation is about being awake. It is a conscious experience in which we practice being present and aware. And, being present and aware does not belong to any one religion, because it is our essential nature. Meditation has no religion. The amazing thing is that although formal religions encourage us to be loving, we still have to experience what it means to *be* loving. Meditation opens the door to loving behavior. As we open and blossom with innate experiences of Awareness—manifesting Curiosity, Gratitude, Compassion, Humor, Creativity, and taking 100% Responsibility in our daily interactions—we have more love to share with our self, our family, and our community.

In meditation, we discover who we are by observing our own hearts and minds. We sit quietly. We listen, breath-by-breath, moment-to-moment, to what's going on. No one else is there to tell us what's real and what's not. We look into it. It is up to us to take Responsibility for tuning into Awareness and being curious about what is happening. We learn through direct inner experience what is loving and what is not.

A meditation practice is always a practical means for cultivating Awareness, regardless of one's religious beliefs. Therefore the idea that one has to be Buddhist to meditate, and by extension Sufi, Hindu, or a member of any other religion that recommends meditation, is incorrect..

MYTH 11: Study Myth

"A meditation practice requires studying religious texts."

My meditation teacher told us reading could get in the way of direct experience of life. I found the advice refreshing and didn't want to read anyway, so that was okay with me. When I wasn't involved in everyday activities like cooking, eating, going to school, or sleeping, I sat in meditation. I went to retreats, and listened to talks about practice. I practiced the practice of meditation, incorporating its gifts into my every day life.

Some years ago, I developed an appetite for reading. Suddenly, spiritual poetry, magazines, and books supported my experience. I realized reading nourished me. Now I understood my teacher's caution against reading. I first needed the taste of my own wisdom, gleaned from my direct experience, and understanding, not someone else's description. What's more, I had to find out for myself how reading *could* get in the way of direct understanding of life, yet, at another time, enhance my understanding!

Some reading can be helpful, of course. Information about how the mind works educates us. Poetry takes us beyond our linear experience of the world. Writings about healthy ways to live and think stimulate our understanding. Writings can inspire us to keep going so that we can know for our self what is true.

It is important, however, to remember that we only find wisdom through our own direct experience. Our understanding will ripen to wisdom only when we go beyond words, and unite our direct experience of Awareness with correct information about *what is*.

What Gets in the Way

MYTH 12: Can't Myth

"I can't do it."

Anyone who wants to meditate can. Some may need to start slowly. Sitting meditation for five minutes in the morning may be just right. Sitting mindfully for five minutes at your desk may be just right. It may be just right to sit in your car and practice focusing on the breath until the light changes. Your daily meditation time may expand without you realizing it.

It can help tremendously to have the support of others engaged in this inner work. Sit with a group on a regular basis if possible. Choosing to sit with other people with an Awareness practice helps to support and inspire us and can be extremely important —especially in the beginning.

It is also extremely helpful to have the personal or group guidance of a meditation teacher. There are many teachers. Teachers may appear in person, in books, CDs, in talks, or on the web. Use your discernment to find a teacher who supports your unfolding. Be open, and notice who appears.

Cultivating a deeply personal interest in freeing yourself from habitual reaction to life, a new world is waiting for you. Your new world is full of clarity, joy, and Compassion. And the ironic thing is, your "new" world has been there all along and that the "can't do it" belief was just another mistaken belief covering up the truth.

A moment of reflection

How do you feel about the list of meditation myths? Do you have a personal favorite to add? If you found yourself in the list, did you find a fresh

What Gets in the Way

perspective? If you have stopped meditating, is there a renewed willingness to try meditation again and stick with it this time around? For those who have not yet begun a meditation practice, did you find yourself more curious about starting one?

Part III

Remembering Who We Really Are

*"We actively retrain our minds
to be focused and aware."*

Chapter Six
Beginning the Journey

Awareness

"Awareness" is a word we often hear in spiritual communities. It is a word used to express the experience of being fully present and conscious in the moment. Being aware is used interchangeably with being awake, present, conscious, attentive, alert, and responsive. The root of aware comes from Old English *gewaer*, which means "watchful." The basis for "waking up," is the practice of Awareness and mindful living.

What is being aware? Aware is when we walk outside after a summer rain shower with a receptive mind, our senses alive with the sensuous embrace of fragrance, birdsong, warmth, and light. If loud, friendly neighbors join us unexpectedly, our welcoming, smiling face greets them—with no sense of interruption, no problem—only openness from head to toe. Awareness is when we feel awake on all levels.

Yet, isn't it true that much of our life, we do not feel awake or aware? We resent other people entering the quiet space we've been enjoying by our self. We get caught up in dreams of things being different; maybe living with someone else, or somewhere else. We feel rushed and go from moment to moment caught up in thoughts of what just happened, or what will happen next. Aren't we often trying to do so many things, our life has become a never-ending to-do list?

Is this working? Do you hear a voice within telling you there is a better way to live your life.

Noticing *what is*

The first step of Awareness is to notice *what is*. Focusing inward, the first thing we may notice is a continual stream of thoughts—opinions, ideas, judgments, and notions about how people and life should be. We frequently confuse our beliefs about how things should be, with things as they *are*. We think other people should be different. We think life should be different. Listen carefully to your thoughts, and find out for yourself if this is true.

Let's look at an example many can relate to, "My child should do better in school." Parents often express this thought, desiring to make a child different, and many of us felt it pressed on us as children. Acknowledging this thought, we become more aware of our own beliefs. Then, perhaps, we can look at a child struggling to keep up in school in the larger context of *what is*. Noticing the child's uniqueness and natural need for attention, family issues, individual learning styles, possible personality conflict with a teacher, and the size of the class— our understanding may expand to include creative ways to help the child succeed in a difficult situation.

I remember that school was a difficult place for me to learn in. I had a difficult time sitting still. If tested with today's standards, I may have been labeled ADHD. My father paid little attention to my school experience until it was time to think about college. Then, he panicked. I realized he had no idea who I was, as he yelled and threatened to lock me in my room to make me study so I could go to Radcliff, Smith, or Vassar. My father was struggling with *what is*. Tremendous pain was created in our relationship at the time because he felt so strongly that I *should* be different.

Noticing thought, clouds moving

The *shoulds* and *shouldn'ts* have been unconscious for so long, we believe they are true and act from them unquestioningly. Seeing people as they really are, the thoughts of wanting someone to be different dissolve in Awareness. To illustrate, we can say that clouds represent thoughts. And blue sky is an unfettered, open, aware mind.

Clouds float across the sky, as thoughts through the mind. Sometimes the clouds are stormy, and sometimes gray, or light and fluffy. Thoughts feel cloudy, stormy, or light as they pass through the mind, don't they? We can learn to let *should*-thoughts, and other pain-producing thoughts, pass through without getting caught up in them. Then we might more often experience the mind as our clear blue sky.

If we simply notice thoughts, without holding onto them or adding anything, thoughts move through the mind without getting stuck. We notice their presence, and notice their movement as they pass by, with no disturbance. Just *what is*. There is nothing to "Velcro" to, no trace is left, just clouds passing by. Whoosh! What a joy!

Different tools of Awareness practice

How do we begin to live with more Awareness? How do we become more present, so we can hear our thoughts and feel our bodies; so we can become more aware of what we are saying, feeling, and doing?

Meditation is the key. In fact, the practice of Awareness is meditation, whether you are sitting in silence, washing dishes, dancing, or driving to work.

Just by returning our attention to the breath we are present, whether we are sitting at the computer, doing yoga, or in the midst of a disagreement.

Sitting meditation can be an enormous gift. We actively retrain our minds to be focused and aware. While sitting with busy mind or quiet mind, experiencing a sense of peace or physical discomfort, we use the time to practice being with *what is*. Meditating regularly, we can focus during the day, and our lives become less stressful. And, sitting in a quiet space, with as few distractions as possible, helps to balance the busy pace of our daily lives.

For beginners, it is recommended to practice sitting Awareness meditation at least 10-15 minutes every day. Over time, you may notice a natural inclination to sit for longer periods. Many people set their clocks earlier and take advantage of the early morning stillness. Others prefer to meditate in the evening before bed. Sitting meditation at the end of the day can quiet the mind and help us ease into sleep with a spacious mind, uncluttered by concerns.

Meditation in both morning and evening is a wonderful gift to give oneself! Try setting up a special spot for meditation in your home. Nothing fancy is necessary. The easiest way to encourage yourself, is to put a chair or cushion in a quiet place. It will remind you of your Intention whenever you pass by.

Awareness eventually takes us into the core of our habitual pain-producing beliefs because it helps us become more aware of our discomfort. Then we can wonder about its cause. Our ability to discern *when* to dig deeper and explore mistaken beliefs develops as we come to recognize the repetitive nature of our painful reactivity. The exploration itself is *what is!* Other times, we recognize a familiar pain-producing thought as it arises, and remember what happened when we got velcroed to it in the past. We can learn to let those thoughts just pass through the mind without attachment.

We also might hear about a "tool" that helps Awareness—such as Counting Judgments Practice, I Can Handle This, Wanting Nothing Practice, Naming Practice, "just this," "I am," and Stop, Look, and Listen Practice— and put them to good use along the way. Even though we can pick up Awareness tools and use them as needed, it can be helpful to check in with a meditation teacher to help us when questions arise about our practice.

The Intention, or motivation, for a life of Awareness is not something one person can give to another. Our desire to grow, our spiritual Longing, comes from our relationship with our self, the people in our life, and our experiences with the body/mind. Each of us must find out for our self what it means to feel whole and be present.

Practicing means practicing with Compassion

In the beginning of our journey to become more aware, we experience Awareness occasionally. It is like the beginning of anything new—whether we're learning to be parents or learning to play a musical instrument—it takes patience and practice. Training the mind to pay attention in a new way also takes practice. Over time, we notice being aware more often.

We also develop the skill of inquiring within to find out what is true. We begin to expand our heart's capacity for Compassion for self and others as our understanding expands. We naturally long for more love, patience, honesty, and clarity in our lives. We begin to notice how our unconscious thoughts, words, and actions can cause us to be unloving, impatient, and dishonest with our self and others. We also begin to feel the petals of our flower opening to the Light of Awareness as we notice Curiosity, Humor, Gratitude, Compassion, 100% Responsibility, and Creativity coming alive in our life.

A natural evolution

The journey of living with Awareness is actually a natural evolution. Our continual pain and confusion is a messenger telling us, "There must be a better way to live!" On the meditation mat, or in a chair, we experience the breath and strengthen our Intention to keep practicing. By practicing living with Awareness and by being with the breath, we discover the life we longed for. Our flower petals open. Sometimes it takes hard work to counter our usually busy, rushing from moment-to-moment life. And it is completely worth it. Cultivating Awareness is incredibly worthwhile work, because Awareness grows more Compassion, clarity, and presence in the world— and our world certainly needs as much of *that* as possible.

Chapter Seven

Awareness and Meditation

1. Taking Five Minutes[30]

You may wish to read this aloud, record it yourself to play back, or have someone read this to you.

Please make yourself comfortable in a sitting position. Intending to listen and focus inwardly, it is best to sit in a comfortable, erect posture. The oxygen and blood get to the brain more easily in this position. The Intention is to be aware, and we are more awake in this posture. Some people have asked about lying down to meditate. It can be wonderful to lay the body down to rest. But, typically, when we lie down, we are programmed to go to sleep or rest deeply.

This work is about being more awake to our life.

So, now you are sitting in an erect posture. Carefully, slowly, look around the space you are in. Take it all in with your eyes. Notice colors, shapes, textures, arrangement, light, and shadow. Notice the sounds around you. Using the eyes and ears, take it all in.

Drawing your Awareness in, think the words—*neck* free, *back* to lengthen and widen. There is nothing to do. Just think those words "*Neck* free, *back* to lengthen and widen." Notice what happens.

Rest your hands gently on the lap, palms facing up, near the belly. If you rest the back of your left hand on top of your right palm, your thumbs will rest

---

[30] The instructions given here are meant to help readers begin a meditation practice. It is recommended that you find a meditation teacher who can answer questions when they arise from your meditation experience. The author's contact information is listed on page VIII in the back of the book.

easily, barely touching tips together. This is a common hand position used in meditation. You may use it if you like.

Now, lower your eyes so they are resting at about a 45-degree angle in front of you. This helps the mind stay more alert. Closing the eyes often denotes sleep and rest to the brain. Cultivating Awareness, it can be helpful to keep the eyes open just a bit; it helps us maintain the inward focus and an alert mind state.

If you are sitting in a chair, feel the feet making contact with the floor. Feel the body making contact with the seat. If you are sitting on cushions on the floor, feel your contact with the floor and cushions. Be aware of your physical sensations for a few moments.

Maintaining your focus, count exhalations to oneself from "one" to "ten." Breathing out say "one" to yourself. Notice breathing in, and upon breathing out, you say, "two to yourself, up to "ten." One exhalation,[31] one number.

Getting to "ten," you go back to "one" and so on. If you forget what number you're on, or get caught up in thought, whenever you remember the counting, you simply go back to "one."

If you lose focus, for any reason, return to "one." It is always the same, again and again. Returning to "one." Some people don't get past "one" and that is okay.

Notice the breath. Follow the inhalation and exhalation wherever you find it in the body— the nostrils, the throat, the chest, the belly, or the whole body. There is no right or wrong way to breathe.

---

[31] It is also fine to count both inhalations and exhalations; one inhalation, "one," one exhalation "two" up to "ten." Some people find this more helpful than counting exhalations only.

Be with the movement of the breath. Simply notice breathing in, and breathing out.

Notice how you treat yourself when you realize you forgot the number, or got lost in thought for a while. That *moment* of noticing how you treat yourself when you make mistakes can give you a full taste of what meditation is about. The job is to notice what is really going on right here. If there is self-judgment you can practice forgiveness and Compassion right here. You might even smile as you acknowledge the human condition that gets so caught up in judging "right" and "wrong" when you make a mistake.

Please be gentle with yourself.

Continue on your own for five minutes.

After sitting

Remember to move slowly, when you are done with a sitting period. Give yourself a moment or two before you start moving. As we first begin to meditate in this way, questions may arise about Intentions, posture, thoughts, fears, pains, or actually anything. It is important to remember that excellent help is available. You just have to ask for it.

In the beginning

In the beginning, some people can't get past "one." It makes no difference. Meditation is a way of practicing remembering to be present. This beginning work of cultivating Awareness with meditation immediately offers you two important gifts. The first gift is to notice how you treat yourself when you believe you made a mistake. Is there tightness when you forget the number you are on, or notice you've counted to thirty? Judgment? A sense of failure? Counting breath meditation practice is not about receiving a grade for a good or bad performance. Can you respond to your inner conflict and smile, and in so doing, send loving kindness to yourself? And then go back to "one." The second gift of this practice is to feel how difficult it can be to pay attention, to stay focused. If we are to be more aware, we need to pay attention.

Counting is an excellent tool to practice staying focused. At some point we may feel counting is no longer useful. There is no right or wrong timing for dropping the counting and simply being with the breath. It's fine to stop counting the breath when we are ready. Tools can be helpful. As soon as they are no longer useful, we just put them down. Actually, tools often fade away without us having to do anything at all. Eventually, tools are not necessary with this work.

There is a story of a Zen master in Japan who used the counting practice his whole life. I got compulsive with counting stairs, steps, and trees, even cracks in the sidewalk! I soon realized following the breath was best for me. Many people follow the breath as a lifetime meditation practice because the breath is always right here, in the moment.

2. Practical Guidance

Breath practice

The breath practice is simply returning our Awareness to our breath. With Awareness, we notice the movement of the breath. As we become distracted and forget our Intention, we return with Awareness again, and again, to the breath. Noticing—without blame and without judgment—forgetting and remembering, forgetting and remembering. And coming back to the work of the moment—noticing the breath as it moves in the body.

Sometimes we can't find the breath's movement in the body. If that happens, try focusing attention on the nostrils and follow the breath as it enters the body. You may also notice pushing to make the breath different. If you find that happening, it may be helpful to notice other body sensations for awhile—the parts of the body making contact with the floor, hands resting on your lap, your posture—and remember that the breath happens without any help from us. Then you can return to noticing the breath without pushing. Breath happens. You can notice it without having to "do" anything, as an impartial, interested, witness of *what is*.

As we practice with the breath, we can get caught up in thought. Stories may hold our attention for a whole round of sitting. In the midst of a story, we may notice that we have gotten caught up in thought. Seeing thoughts as clouds that pass through the mind frees us from our story, and allows us to rest again in Awareness of the breath.

Thoughts have no power unless we "catch a ride on them" and let them take us away from this moment. Remember, sometimes the sky is dark with storm clouds, or filled with light fluffy shapes, or quick-moving wind-blown streaks in the sky. Sitting here, being here now, we experience first hand the work of *being here now*. Breath practice is the work of returning, returning to the breath, returning our attention to this moment, again and again.

Whole body listening

Can you imagine listening with the whole body? In fact, the practice of Awareness is exactly that— a listening to *what is* with the whole body. Instead of focusing on the breath alone, some prefer full body listening practice.[32] During meditation, we have an opportunity to listen differently—in a fresh way, with sparkling Energy and clarity—directing our focus as if the whole body can hear and we are tremendously curious about what's being said.

Often when we're listening to someone speak, or just sitting in silence, we are engaged in an inner conversation. As thoughts pass through the mind, we get caught up in them. Questions arise about tomorrow's dinner or yesterday's argument. The children. The laundry. On and on. Have you noticed this happening?

Listening with the whole body, we practice listening in a new way, as if the whole body was one great big ear focusing inward. As thoughts come up our focus returns to the listening within. We bring our attention to our inner experience *as it is*. As discomfort arises, we listen with Awareness and Curiosity, directing our focus right into the area that feels discomfort.

Feeling open, relaxed, and present, we can listen deeply. Staying focused on someone speaking to us, we might also let sounds, thoughts, and sensations pass through us. Remaining unattached to any experience—both pleasurable and uncomfortable—helps us stay focused on the speaker's words and open to *what is*.

---

[32] Because we have two ears and generally think of ears as the only organ of hearing, some people have difficulty with the suggestion to listen with the whole body. When I first explored this practice, I imagined giant ears on the side of my head to help me focus my listening skills within. I no longer need the visualization to help me focus. Using our imagination can be a gift when we use it to help us focus. And like other tools, we can stop using it when it's no longer useful.

Listening fully, with the whole body. Focusing inward. Listening. Quietly. No pushing, no blaming. Just listening. Listening to breath. Listening to thoughts, as they arise. Listening to sounds. Birds singing, mowers, cars, rain on the roof. House creaking. Heart beating. Breathing. Sensations arising, and subsiding.

Listening like this is a way of careful noticing, and is not about changing anything. It is not about pushing or trying to make anything different. It is the quality of seeing/hearing things as they really are. Nothing else to "do." Just noticing *what is*.

Pain in meditation

Are you familiar with the colorful woven grass toy where the pointer finger on each hand goes into each end of the toy? Once the fingers are inside, they get stuck if you try to pull them out. The trick is to figure a way to get the fingers out. The harder you pull to free the fingers, the tighter the hold gets on the fingers. In order to free the fingers you need to relax, push the fingers slightly together, and then gently slide them out—which is the exact opposite of what you naturally want to do. It is the same way with pain. We naturally want it to go away. We unconsciously pull away from it, tighten around it and then try to push it away. Does fighting with pain work?

Letting go of habitual responses to pain during meditation, is just like seeing how to get our stuck fingers out of a toy. Noticing sensations, noticing how fighting pain makes things tighter, can we wonder about how to be with pain differently?

One way is to inquire directly into the experience of pain, asking, "What is this?" Sincerely asking this question, openly with no expectation, a shift in the experience of the pain occurs, and we experience sensation with Awareness. Our instinct to react by tightening, and pulling away, is interrupted by Awareness.

Also, bringing a gentle attention to our pain, simply focusing our attention on the sensations without actually naming it pain, something changes our experience of it. Our Curiosity is aroused and we begin to be aware of sensations on a different level.

Working with Awareness, the need to push discomfort away may dissolve. The pain may lessen its impact on the body/mind, or increase in intensity. As our attention stays focused we are better able to handle the discomfort. We may notice sensations shifting and possibly going away. We may also notice pain that points to further exploration with a health professional. It is possible and loving to respond to pain in a new way.

3. A Few Words about Teachers

The stuff in the attic

Unfamiliar and uncomfortable sensations and memories can arise with a meditation practice. As we cultivate Awareness, we naturally become more conscious of what has been ignored, denied, and pushed away. Awareness includes the uncomfortable stuff we've "hidden in our attic." And because we usually need to feel discomfort in order to grow, this stuff is actually a hidden treasure. We can use it as fertilizer for our blossoming.

One of the challenges in the beginning is that we can feel isolated, as though no one else understands or cares about what we're going through. With activated Intentions, and Curiosity aroused, this painful stuff can lead us to discover that we are not alone. We are fortunate to be alive in a time when so many teachers are available and freely sharing their insights and experiences. Besides countless books, CDs, and DVDs, there is also a large amount of useful information about Awareness and meditation on the Internet. In addition, many meditation teachers offer personal guidance and retreats. Spending time with an authentic meditation teacher can be of great assistance when we're ready to explore what's been "hidden in the attic."

An awake meditation teacher guides us to see beyond our stories, to a direct experience of what's real, and what's loving. They demonstrate a fresh perspective with their words, and their actions. They invite us to join them because they *know* the clarity, compassion, and presence is possible for all of us. And they know from experience that the work of opening of heart and mind is worth it.

Noticing guidance

An old woman's home sits in the middle of a terrible flood. She goes out on her porch as the water rises, and sees a boat full of people going by. They call out to her, offering help. "No thank you," she shouts back, " I trust that God will save me."

As the water gets higher, she goes up to the second floor, and opens a window to see another boat, with people offering help. Again, she says, "No thank you. I trust that God will save me."

Sitting up on the roof, a helicopter flies over to her, to offer her help. Still, her answer is, "No thank you, I trust that God will save me."

The woman dies in the flood, and when she gets to heaven, she feels angry with God. She meets God and demands to know why God didn't save her. God answered, "What do you think I was doing? I sent people to help you three times?!?"

Unlike the woman in the above humorous story, when we are curious and willing to take Responsibility for making things better, we can notice guidance and move toward it. Guidance gets easier to notice as we cultivate Awareness. In reality, everyone and everything we meet provides guidance. We just have to notice it. An impatient parent reminds us to be patient with our children, a driver cutting us off on the highway reminds us how important it is to be attentive every moment, and a neighbor who offers to help digging us out after a blizzard shows us we are not alone—when we pay attention.

With a meditation practice, we become better at being present. With Awareness, we notice how being velcroed to our story keeps us from experiencing the full blossoming of our being. Becoming even more familiar with our inner voices and stories, our understanding deepens. Throughout our process of waking up, we filter what is personally useful from what is not. We may realize that attachment to our stories is the underlying problem in all relationships with self and others. At some point, we may feel a pull towards getting some personal assistance with our practice.

A relationship with a teacher is not about blind trust. We need to find out if what the teacher says is true for us. We may need to spend some time with what is being suggested before we know if it's a fit or not. Staying open, in spite of our confusion, is the key. With openness and curiosity aroused, we can experiment with suggestions. Although Awareness helps our discernment develop, sometimes it can be years before we fully understand what our teacher has pointed out. And that's okay.

Just talking about what works is not enough. Spiritual teachers live their own unique expression of a fully blossoming human being. We can notice the qualities of joy, presence, and compassion in their actions. They mirror our possibilities. A teacher's spontaneous actions, words, and presence in our life can be a gift beyond measure.

Meditation teachers share their experience and wisdom as a gift to serve humanity. Through their direct experience and personal understanding they have found out what is true and what is not. Even though all meditation teachers are human and make mistakes, an authentic teacher will always direct us to find out what is true and what is not, through our own experience.

We need to keep going

Doing this deep work, the meaning of the word meditation expands beyond sitting still time. We learn about sitting still and quieting the mind. We continue to cultivate more presence with "everyday mind." We understand from our own experience that growth is a process. Perhaps we want to go deeper. We know we have just begun a journey.

From the beginning of our practice, learning to embrace the difficult, as well as the wonderful, means learning about being with *what is*. The direct experience with our habitually fearful judgments and self-criticizing thoughts challenges us.

We realize that it is our Responsibility to find a new relationship with our pain-producing habits.

Teachers help us figure out what practice is best for us. They help us explore what is best when we are unsure or feel stuck and ask for help. Our practice may change over time. Different meditation practices can help us along the way, when we stay focused, and practice, practice, practice. The important thing is that we keep going.

It can be valuable to remember the interplay between all the petals of our developing Flower of Inner Growth. Then, we can experience Humor with Awareness and remember Compassion for our self, as we occasionally forget, and drift away from our daily practice. Our lack of Compassion for others reminds us that we are not being aware. Curiosity about going deeper reminds us of Awareness, meditation practice, and exploring our beliefs. Creativity shows us *how* to keep going when we feel stuck and get caught up in our pain-producing beliefs again and again.

Taking 100% Responsibility for our behavior redirects our attention when we are looking outside of our self for the cause of our discontent. Gratitude naturally arises and inspires us to keep going as we notice how we have changed. We become more loving as mistaken beliefs fall way and presence takes their place. We practice because we know there are benefits from our direct experience with meditation and Awareness. At some point we know we *have* to keep going. The quality of our life depends upon it.

Part IV

The Adventure

*"You only get it when you are halfway there.
 If you find you've gone all the way,
Keep going."*

Dōgen

Chapter Eight
Being Open With All of It

Gayle's story

Gayle had been coming to me for Qi Gong[33] healing for several years. The first time I asked her if she meditated her response was immediate.

"I'm a great meditator!" Gayle had exclaimed with a smile on her face.

She had often mentioned her meditation in the past, and always made it clear her practice was about relaxation. Gayle would put on some nice music and lie down. Her mind would quiet down and she would feel deeply relaxed. Gayle said her relaxing meditation kept her going.

This time, as Gayle was getting ready to leave after her Qi Gong session, she shared more about her current reasons for scheduling a session. Her elderly mother had been hospitalized for a month with cancer and couldn't keep food down. In addition, Gayle and her sister shared the care of their father, who was house bound, on tube feeding. Gayle was greatly stressed and reached out by calling me. She knew a Qi Gong session would help her relax and relieve her chronic back pain. I asked Gayle if she'd been meditating, especially considering the amount of stress in her life.

"No, I haven't been able to. Once I lie down and turn on my music, my thoughts about my parents and all start up, and I'm out of there! If I can't relax there is no reason to torture myself trying."

I mentioned to Gayle another way to think about her meditation time. I suggested that she use it to notice the thoughts that created more stress. "Gayle,"

---
[33] See footnote on page 22.

The Adventure

I said, "Instead of giving up when stressful thoughts take over, listen to them with Curiosity. Notice what happens in the body when these thoughts take over. Allow the busy, stress creating thoughts to pass through the mind as clouds pass through a clear blue sky. Let them pass through without getting all caught up in them, or velcroed to them!"

"Hmmm. Sounds interesting," Gayle said, "You mean I don't have to be a perfect, calm, meditator?"

"No," I smiled, "Not all the time. Gayle, how about practicing being the Quiet in The Center of Chaos?"

"I'm more like the Hurricane in The Center of the Chaos," she joked.

"Okay," I said, "Try this. When you meditate, stay with whatever comes up no matter how chaotic the weather. Notice what's happening. Just bring your Curiosity to whatever thoughts and feelings arise. It can be like watching the weather changing outside your window. You will develop the skill of staying with whatever comes up in your life."

Gayle looked curious so I continued, "Practice being in the moment, instead of stressing about what just happened or what you imagine will be next. Okay?"

"I still need my music." Gayle added.

"Music is fine," I said. "How about sitting for 10 minutes in silence, with the simple Intention of being aware of *what is*? Then, listen to music and do your relaxation. That way, you can have the best of both worlds. You are training the mind to focus in the moment, you are noticing what comes up, and you have relaxation time as well." Gayle looked happy as she realized that she didn't have

The Adventure

to give up one to have the other kind of meditation. "And besides," I added, "I think your music relaxation time will be more enjoyable after the ten minutes of Quiet in The Center of Chaos."

"Sounds great," laughed Gayle.

After we hugged goodbye, I noticed a look of confusion on Gayle's face. "Any questions?" I asked.

Gayle said, "What do I do when my thoughts get <u>real</u> busy?" She needed a specific tool to help focus her new meditation practice, so I suggested a counting breath practice for the ten-minute session. I mentioned the counting might drop away after a time.

Gayle was enthusiastic as she walked away. "I'm going to try this tonight. I am so excited!"

Gayle's impulse to meditate was stimulated by the pain in her family life. That pain helped her take the first step on her new adventure, towards a deeper connection with her inner life.

Why people meditate

Curiosity about our pain opens the door to going deeper. But what brings a person to the point where they want to meditate and are *ready* to sit still and tune into their inner world?

I have noticed three reasons why people begin a meditation practice:

1. To relax.

2. To relieve their mental, emotional, physical, and spiritual pain and in order to know who they really are.

3. To help relieve the suffering of others.

All three reasons are interdependent and will eventually include the other two. For example, taking time to sit still and experience the breath, not pushing, or "doing" anything, just noticing *what is*, the body/mind feels better and relaxes. We may begin to remember focusing on our breath for a moment in the midst of stressful situations. Over time, we experience the busy-ness of our life with less pain and confusion. As we take better care of our self, we help others, and change the world. No matter what brings us to meditation, it is a good thing.

A fresh perspective

Gayle's experience of quieting down with music helped her to be more open to a new perspective about meditation. She had previously experienced benefits from meditating her way, yet what she was doing wasn't relaxing because of her extremely stressful family situation. Her Curiosity grew about what else could help her. The mental, physical, and emotional strain of caring for her aging parents forced her to go deeper. She needed something new and was ready for a fresh perspective about meditation.

I remember the moment that I knew I wanted to go deeper. I was attending a retreat with Toni Packer at the Rochester Zen Center. During a talk to the group, she posed the question, "Do you want to be like your parents?" Upon hearing Toni's question, every cell in the body resonated with a screaming, "No!" At our next private meeting, Toni and I spoke about a new practice to fit my profound sense of urgency.

The Adventure

Wanting to be helpful

A natural development of a meditation practice is becoming more aware of how our behaviors affect others. As I cultivated more Awareness, I noticed the effects of my angry explosions on my family, and I naturally wanted to stop hurting them. I knew there was a way to stop, even if I'd have to work hard to do it.

I also became more aware of the tremendous suffering around me. There are endless opportunities to be of service to others every day. It is a gift to be able to help others in small ways, greeting people with a smile while doing errands around town, bringing kindness to a business meeting, volunteering in the community, or offering help to friends who are moving.

During meditation, we focus in a loving, and non-judgmental way with the body/mind. We become more sensitive to the times when we push, ignore, and fight the body's experience. We learn that being with *what is*, is more loving than fighting or pushing away what is happening. Physically, we tend to want to eat better and get more exercise. We gradually learn the gift of self-care and generally, we feel better. As our experience of Awareness grows, we also become less affected by outer circumstances.

With Awareness, our emotional life comes into Balance as we discover mistaken beliefs and explore them. As we learn more about how the body/mind works, we deal better with stress and are more helpful to others. Our petals open and communicate well together.

The Adventure

Working with change

As we touched upon previously, Gayle was ready for a fresh perspective. Standing together and talking at our front door, she listened intently. At the time, I could tell that something was resonating for Gayle and she was becoming curious about a new possibility instead of giving up on meditation all together. In a way, all the pain in Gayle's life was a blessing. She was open to a completely fresh way of seeing things. She was becoming curious about another way to meditate. Even though she was drawn to new information, Gayle also, naturally, wanted to hold on to what felt comfortable.

Sometimes change happens in baby steps. Other times, it can be dramatic. And, it doesn't matter whether it is baby steps or giant leaps. Change happens anyway.

What is interesting is that we resist change whenever fear or judgments fill the mind. After all, change is the last thing our ego[34] wants. Unless we question the *status quo* when beliefs make us uncomfortable, we remain with the way we are, because we're comfortable with the known. In fact, how often do we hear a great new possibility and argue against it just because it is change?

Are you familiar with the struggle between what you intuitively know is best and what your ego tells you? One Zen master said the best way to deal with tension from this struggle is to choose the opposite of what the ego wants. The ego says, "I've got to have music right now," so you drive with the silence. The ego says, "Yummy cake…mmmm. Have another piece!" so you choose to

---

[34] The word ego, as it is meant here, points to the aspect of self that includes our beliefs, personality, and identification with a separate sense of the self we call "I." It has been conditioned from birth. Unless we question the pain-filled mistaken reality of the ego, we remain confused and in conflict with the way things really *are*.

forego cake right then. Or the ego says, "I've got to tell him a thing or two right now," and you decide against it. Practicing the simple "rule of doing the opposite" is a stimulating practice (used with discretion), and can open doors to a healthier life. Try this for a day and you may discover much about yourself.

Being flexible

As it was for Gayle, it is loving to be flexible when we want to learn something new. We know the first step of change is often the most difficult. The good news is change gets easier over time. As we become more familiar with the voices of ego that create our confusion and suffering, we learn to move with Creativity and loving feelings instead. There is a direct connection between our meditation practice and being more compassionate, clear, and patient. We want to practice because we feel a difference in our life. It is that simple.

A new inner landscape had opened up for Gayle, and she was moving willingly and joyfully towards it. Gayle was enthused with a sense of adventure. Her new meditation is being with and exploring Awareness. Gayle will cultivate Awareness, whether she sits, lies with her back on the floor, or stands while meditating. Gayle may also be more open to change instead of struggling and fighting against it. Her openness to change was created by a natural desire to relieve her suffering. As the Awareness of her painful family situation joined with Curiosity, activated good Intentions, and Energy, she was willing to try something new.

The Adventure

Gayle's adventure begins

Hearing from Gayle a month later, she told me she loved her new meditation practice. She asked her husband and son to leave her alone before she meditated. She started with ten minutes and was up to an hour sometimes. She had more Energy for her parents, her work, her family, and herself. I noticed she looked years younger, her facial muscles had so deeply relaxed from the last time I saw her. She said she was continuing to meditate because it helped her have more Energy and presence in the "Center of Chaos." Interestingly, she had stopped listening to music during her meditation time.

Gayle may notice changes in people around her too. Over time, she may connect her Awareness meditation practice with her ability to be more loving, and realize the interconnection between Awareness practice and helping others. Most importantly, if she keeps going, Gayle's personal experience will weave all three reasons for meditation into her life.

The real adventure

Usually we reserve our sense of adventure for worldly explorations; caves, mountains, rivers, a new city, new job, or new people. Turning our attention inward, to the infinitely creative inner life, requires a sense of adventure as well. The inner life is inexhaustible and full of riches. Your Flowering of Inner Growth is with you on every adventure. Bringing a sense of wonder and enthusiasm to this inner exploration, you will have an adventure filled with joy, clarity, Compassion, Humor, and Creativity.

The Adventure

Making meditation a part of your life is, in a sense, a lone adventure. Each of us must do our inner work so that we can live with Awareness. We do it alone or in groups. It may be helpful to think of the word "alone" as "all one." We are actively engaged in embracing the many voices, the many stories, and learning about being in the absolute, immediate present as a fully integrated, whole, "all one" human being.

Fortunately, we are also on this adventure with everyone else. Spending time with people who support our practice, are growing in Awareness themselves, and understand we are all in this together, inspires us to keep going. However, our contact with others provides a different kind of support for our growth, a kind of fertilizer (think of fertilizer as the experiences we have in life that help us blossom). This fertilizer is often filled with unpleasant, painful experiences and memories, which provide us with perpetually fresh material (more fertilizer) to continue the exploration of what is loving and what is not.

We transform our life by the attitude and Awareness we bring to our fertilizer. Enthusiastic Curiosity breaks open the resistance that habit places in the way. Nothing can stand in the way of energized Curiosity. Questioning, deeply longing to understand *what this is*, we live the adventure, being more present, as our life flows from moment-to-moment.

No one has to remind us to Stop, Look, and Listen. It is a focus we willingly accept out of a deeply felt desire for our full blossoming. We have learned the necessity of Awareness through our experience. We have surrendered to the need for meditation to help us stay awake in our daily life. Our deepest desire is to live from our wholeness, the true blossoming of one life in the midst of it all.

The Adventure

This inner adventure is worthy of enthusiasm. It is full of fears to overcome. It is full of humorous and scary mistakes, and challenges at every turn. Our adventure often requires moment-to-moment detailed attention to what is right in front of us. Meditation is the vehicle of the adventure. Our Awareness defines the quality of our experience. It is simple and it is the adventure of a lifetime. Actually, it is the real adventure of *this* lifetime.

The Adventure

May you fully express the flowering of your Inner Growth.
May you uncover
The Great Gifts
of
Curiosity, Humor, Creativity, Responsibility, Gratitude,
and
Compassion
On your adventure.
May your adventure bring you,
and
Everyone else in your life,
Happiness.
May you come into contact with,
and
Be open to,
Correct information and compassionate guidance
to
Help you along the way.

Author's Note

This book adds only one tiny piece to countless volumes written throughout the ages about awareness and meditation. There is much left unsaid here. As the editing progressed, it became clear that there was always something else that could be said. The focus remained throughout, however, on readers who were fairly new to the information being presented. Therefore, we, meaning the author and her editors, were diligent in walking the fine line between what felt like just enough or too much being offered. We hope we struck a good balance.

Any questions or concerns that arise about aspects of reality not addressed, language that feels unclear, and complex issues that feel oversimplified can be addressed in sincere, and open dialogue. I honor the infinitely varied ways to say what we have also attempted to say. Please feel free to contact me with questions and concerns about what has been offered here.

Padme Nina Livingstone
August 8, 2006

Acknowledgements

I am quite certain that this book has had its own creative energy. Everyone involved, consciously or unconsciously, were only servants in *the book's* plan to be published. I feel deeply grateful to be a part of such a great team of people brought together by whatever unseen creative forces were at work.

Three women were essential to my writing and deserve recognition. I remember the day my high school English teacher sent us home for a two week Christmas break with an assignment to write one composition on anything for each day we were out of school. Having to come up with subjects by myself was terrifying. My mother, who rarely stepped in to help with schoolwork, offered to sit with me each night and go over my work. "Just write like you speak!" she said again and again. "Read it out loud and listen to how it sounds!" My mom taught me how to put my thoughts on paper that vacation. Forty years later, Jo Valerie saw a brochure I had written and encouraged me to write for her magazine *Nature's Wisdom*. And then, my friend Sue Staropoli helped me with extensive editing for my first published article called Growing Gratitude from Weeds, most of which appears in this book under Gratitude. Thank you, thank you, thank you.

Margaret Braun's inspirational guidance and writing expertise helped me get the first words on paper when this book was merely a good title. Margaret was always there with generous, unconditional, support as the writing continued. Her commitment to readability helped keep the writing focused for the reader throughout our time working together. As the initial and long-term editor, she often provided organizational wisdom, syntax, and the perfect word when I was at a loss.

My precious husband, Bill, took over when Margaret and I moved on. In spite of his busy work schedule, soccer, and significant family commitments, he read, reread, edited, and talked about the book with me because I needed his help. Bill's insightful editing helped to keep the writing true. His editing notes often included, "Is this what you (really) want to say?" "Too heady," or "What does this mean?" In the deepest sense, this book could not have been written without him. With a full heart, thank you, Bill.

The following people began as my "readers" and became meaningful editors, to my pleasant surprise. They each gave their time and hearts to the project freely. Sandy Robinson provided the counterpoint every writer needs, to remember that not everyone will love the book. Her few edits were worthwhile as well. Dr. Bruce Freedberg is a dear friend who lived in our home when we were all much younger and members of the Zen Center. His cheerful additions helped add more warmth, humor and clarity, as only Bruce can. Dr. Heather Daly's detailed editing brought the nearly final edition of the book up to snuff, bringing a sense of wholeness to the manuscript that was waiting for her expertise and experience. I am especially grateful to Dr. Daly for putting so much personal time into the book.

Deborah Wright, a knowledgeable and skilled acupuncturist, offered much needed assistance with the difficult task of encapsulating one aspect of Eastern Medicine in a few words. Thank you, Deborah. Your assistance was perfect. Feeling pressure about the inside jacket cover text, I asked a few friends for feedback, which they gave generously. Thank you Bob Brown, Margaret Braun, Marjorie Crum, and Les Morgan. Your timely, insightful aid in my hour of need was greatly appreciated.

Something must be said about my teachers. The people in my family have been my greatest teachers. No words can adequately describe the depth of gratitude I have for my family of birth's loving me enough and providing the perfect fertilizer for my blossoming. So even though you've been gone for a long time, thank you, Mom and Dad. And thank you, Michael, may your life be filled with loving-kindness.

My children are experts at softening my edges. They always bring me back to remembering love and being open. And so, I thank you, Emily and Jason for expanding my heart beyond its known borders, again and again. My husband, Bill, besides being a perfect husband/editor, continually reminds me who I want to be, who I don't want to be, and who I am. You are my dearest friend/partner/teacher for life.

I thank the spiritual teachers who have been there for me in person, in spirit, and through their writings. I thank Roshi Kapleau for his invisible presence and palpable support; Toni Packer for her personal guidance, and especially for "showing the way" through her impeccable use of the English language; Shunryu Susuki Roshi, Pema Chödrön, Thich Nhat Hanh, Byron Katie, Rumi, His Holiness Dalai Lama, and Jack Kornfield, for every word of truth, wisdom, and beauty that you put to paper for those of us who are willing to find out for ourselves.

I am deeply grateful to the clients and friends who contributed so much to my understanding. Jennifer gave permission for me to use her and Maddy's names for their story.[35] Everyone else gave permission to use their story as long as I changed their name, which I did. Thank you all.

From the pure goodness of her heart, Jennifer Prusak contributed her time, energy, and graphic gifts to make the book cover as beautiful as it is. Thank you again, Jennifer.

I have a special note of gratitude for the two artists who generously contributed their fine artwork as gifts. Jacqueline Murray knew only of the Flowering of Inner Growth when I asked for her help. The book was merely a thought then. She whipped out her beautiful watercolor flower as I stood by her side in her kitchen, and I will be forever grateful for her heartfelt generosity. Gretchen Targee has shared her heart and art with me for many lifetimes and there is no way to thank her enough. I sat sipping tea, as Gretchen created, with ink and her wonderful brushes, the four illustrations for the book. I especially loved watching the creation of the black splotch for Part II. It was so simple! And perfect. Just like being a good friend. Finally, I feel endless gratitude for all beings who are working to make this world a better place, one awakening person at a time.

---

[35] Maddy died peacefully on December 1, 2004, surrounded by her loving family, caring friends, and nurturing hospital staff.

Illustrations

Cover: Jacqueline Murray, watercolor artist

Gretchen Targee, artist, mother, and dear friend, contributed all four illustrations for the quotes:

Part I: "And nothing is in the way."
Part II: "Awareness is not always pretty."
Part III: "We actively retrain our minds to be focused and aware."
Part IV: "You only get it when you are halfway there. If you find you've gone all the way, keep going." Dōgen

Quote for Part IV Illustration

Part IV: Zen Master Dōgen, retrieved from Zen-Forum, December 11, 2005, Web site: http://www.zen-forum.com/a22/b2001/c01/d4/e6/z7

A Short List of Related Reading

The Three Pillars of Zen, Philip Kapleau, Roshi
A timeless treasure for people interested in excellent meditation instruction, as well as the basic teachings about Zen Buddhism.

The Wonder of Presence, Toni Packer
Inspirational, instructional, and loving teaching about awareness.

A Path with Heart, Jack Kornfield
An excellent follow-up to this book for those ready to read more about "the perils and promises of spiritual life."

Zen Mind Beginner's Mind, Shunryu Suzuki
Classic meditation instruction, many people's first book

Peace is Every Step, Thich Nhat Hanh
Simple, concise every day awareness practice

Who Dies?, Stephen & Ondrea Levine
Helpful, clear, loving information about death and dying

The Art of Happiness, H.H. Dalai Lama and Howard C. Coulter, M.D.
Just what the title says, with guidance by an expert

Loving What Is, Byron Katie
Exceptional instructions for seeing through all painful belief patterns

The Essential Rumi, Coleman Barks
Poetry/teachings of a spiritual master, lover of life

New and Selected Poems, Volumes One and Two, Mary Oliver
Poetry with attention to detail, awareness & amazement

The Essential Teachings of Ramana Maharshi
Awareness, awareness, awareness by an absolute master

CDs by Padme Nina Livingstone

A Forgiveness Meditation

Forgiving makes space in the heart for peace. It brings peace to painful relationships: disagreements at work, after family conflicts, regrets when a loved one dies, estranged siblings, a difficult divorce, and when there's self-judgment and shame. Listen to Padme or her husband, Bill, as you find forgiveness for self and others. It's a gentle, loving, healing journey.

Uncovering Compassion

Take a journey into the heart of compassion. Padme shares a talk with three guided meditations, which help us nurture compassion with our self... and others. She also gives a talk about what gets in the way of our natural expression of the heart, and has included a 20 minute timed silent meditation period.

Remembering Awareness

Learn about the gifts of awareness and follow guided awareness meditation instructions. There is a 10 minute timed meditation period included.

Available online through www.healingwithawareness.com

Contact information

info@healingwithawareness.com
www.healingwithawareness.com
585.234.0800